Crimesafe g

Also by Edwin Shaw
(with Alan Blows)

Crime in Britain
(Charles Knight Publishing, 1991)

CRIMESAFE GUIDE

Edwin Shaw

Constable · London

First published in Great Britain 1993
by Constable & Company Ltd
3 The Lanchesters, 162 Fulham Palace Road,
London W6 9ER
Copyright © 1993 Edwin Shaw
The right of Edwin Shaw to be
identified as the author of this work
has been asserted by him in accordance
with the Copyright, Designs and Patents Act 1988
ISBN 0 09 472280 3
Set in Sabon 10½pt by
Rowland Phototypesetting Ltd
Bury St Edmunds, Suffolk
Printed in Great Britain by
St Edmundsbury Press Ltd
Bury St Edmunds, Suffolk

A CIP catalogue record for this book
is available from the British Library

The author

Edwin Shaw was born in 1954. After graduating from
Sussex University, he gained a Master's degree in
Philosophy at the London School of Economics. He has
worked as a journalist for various newspapers
including *The Times* and *Sunday Telegraph*, in Britain
and abroad. His previous book, *Crime in Britain*, was
the first to provide detailed information on policing
and crime trends for every region of the country.

In 1986, in Dublin, he was given a Hennessy Award
for Literature for short stories written under a
pseudonym.

An extra-mural tutor for the University of London,
he lives in north London with Rita Goddard and their
baby daughter, Joanna.

Contents

Acknowledgements

I would like to thank the following:

Editorial and Research Assistant: Rita Goddard

Researcher and Contributor: Glen Warren

Crime Prevention advisers: Diana Lamplugh (Suzy Lamplugh Trust), Bert Dady (Metropolitan Police), Chris McCartney (Thatcham Motor Insurance Repair Research Centre)

CIPFA (Chartered Institute of Public Finance and Accountancy), especially Sue Wren, and the Institute for the Study of Drug Dependence.

CIPFA (Chartered Institute of Public Finance and Accountancy), especially Sue Wren, and the Institute for the Study of Drug Dependence.

Advisers have contributed in a purely technical capacity. Any general opinions in the text about institutions or public policy are mine alone.

E.S.

Foreword

No one wants to become a victim of crime. Certainly those who have become a victim of crime realize, very often too late, how devastating it can be. Others allow fear of becoming a victim to cloud their lives. Still more feel that not to think about it at all will ensure their safety.

We, the British public, tend to fall into three camps when it comes to the mention of crime:

1. The fear-bound: 'Isn't life awful, I'm terrified to go out.'
2. The fear-free: 'Crime happens to others, not to me (or those I love).'
3. The fear-less: 'Crimes against the person happen less often than the media would have us believe. On the other hand, property crime is no joke and the threat against personal safety is worrying. I'm going to make sure I think ahead and am prepared on either count.'

Crimes will, and do, happen to all these groups of people. However, it is those who 'fear less' who will have much more chance of avoiding criminal intent and will suffer less if anything does occur. In the experience of the Suzy Lamplugh Trust, people who are enabled to look at the reality of these risks, and who have built their judgements and consequent actions on informed knowledge, will consider any necessary avoidance as mature rather than wimpish. If there should be a crisis we find they are better able to react well at the time and recover much more quickly than those who had hidden their heads in the sand and shut themselves away.

The Suzy Lamplugh Trust aims to empower people to live safer lives. This book will be of great value in the pursuit of a Crimesafe life. It is practical, straightforward, filled with up-to-date information and, above all, easy to read.

Edwin Shaw has done a splendid job. I am delighted that

he has not shied away from tackling the real issues which the government needs to face and the present problems experienced by the police. He discusses the requirements for making the country a safer place which are not being met, the knowledge which is available now but which is not being used, and the abilities which are around but which are not being tapped.

This book puts the whole picture in the frame. *Crimesafe* offers all individuals the chance to help themselves to be free from fear of crime; *Crimesafe* challenges the government to ensure that there are fewer victims of crime; *Crimesafe* sets the police targets for clearing up crime. The Suzy Lamplugh Trust feels everyone will benefit from reading this book and acting upon its recommendations.

My daughter, Suzy, disappeared seven years ago and is now presumed dead. She left me a legacy. When I said goodbye to her after her last home visit, she said, 'Life is for living, mum. Never forget that.' I never have. That is why I welcome this book as an invaluable help to every one of us. However, I also look forward to the next edition and hope it can reflect a country in which we all feel safer.

Diana Lamplugh, OBE
May 1993

1. Introduction

'I don't think I've ever known a period when people have been more concerned and distressed about crime and safety. In fact I can't remember a time when there's been more going on in the field and less comprehension of the real issues . . .' The man who spoke these words is a senior police officer. In making these remarks he identified some of the perplexity and anguish which many people currently feel when they consider the linked questions of crime, law enforcement and safety.

Over the last decade recorded crime has grown hugely. So has the individual's sense of helplessness in the face of it. Enormous attention has also been given to the matter of police corruption and latterly to the prospect of a major reform of policing. Such discussion has been accompanied by wide media coverage of a number of criminal justice scandals.

The police themselves are disillusioned by the way in which the courts operate and by the approach that society takes in dealing with offenders. They feel that sentencing policy is confused, and that the public paradoxically want them to be simultaneously 'low-key' and highly forceful in their operational style.

They are also extremely unhappy with government's planned changes to their organizational structures and conditions of service. In the midst of this constant change, confusion and acrimony, individuals are left with the problem of dealing with their own security. The problem is made even worse by the complicated and bewildering nature of both the security industry and law enforcement agencies.

This book tries to help people get round these problems. First it looks at issues of crime, policing and security in their full political and social context. Secondly it allows readers to consider security questions in the proper framework of risk assessment and policing. We believe it is not possible for people to assess their own security needs properly without examining the full range of relevant factors.

Readers should first of all look at the section on Crime Risks. This will allow them to judge their own personal risk levels. Having done this they should then consult the appropriate parts of the three main sections on Personal Safety, Home Security and Car Crime. The section on Policing should also be consulted each time so that 'a feel' is gained for the many policing issues that directly affect all aspects of crime and safety.

In each of the main sections readers will find background material, covering social and other 'contextual' aspects of the subject, additional material illustrating the more dramatic implications of the topics covered, and also the detailed crime and safety information itself. We cover England, Scotland and Wales, but not Northern Ireland. The special circumstances pertaining in that part of the world place it beyond the scope of this book.

To repeat what was said earlier: readers should first of all decide their own level of risk, and should then use this as a guide to exactly how much security they need in personal or domestic terms. Above all they should try to consider security in context: in the context of risk, policing and changing administrative and governmental policy. The aim is to encourage readers to think for themselves and to make their own choices about their own safety.

Note: all crime and policing statistics in this book are derived from the Home Office, unless otherwise stated.

CRIMESAFE QUIZ
Compiled by Rita Goddard

Try the following quiz and see how much you know about crime and safety. Then look up the answers on p. 257. Whatever your score in the quiz, reading *Crimesafe* will make you better informed and thus better able to make practical choices about areas of pressing importance.

1. What proportion of males born in 1953 has been convicted of a criminal offence?
   a. 1 in 10
   b. 1 in 3
   c. 1 in 13
2. Rape outside the home is a common crime. True or false?
3. Outward-opening doors are:
   a. more vulnerable than inward-opening doors
   b. less vulnerable
   c. outward and inward-opening doors are equally vulnerable
4. Which of the following methods or implements is most used in the murder of females?
   a. blunt instrument
   b. strangulation
5. Which of the following is most likely to be suspected of murdering a woman?
   a. lover or former lover
   b. spouse, cohabitant or former spouse or cohabitant
6. Which of these cars, according to government figures, is most likely to be stolen? Rank in order of risk, medium/high/low.
   a. Triumph Dolomite
   b. Ford Escort Mark 1
   c. Ford Escort Mark 3
   d. Porsche 911
7. Which of these weapons is most used by criminals (excluding licensing offences)? Rank in order of use.
   a. pistol
   b. sawn-off shot-gun
   c. rifle
   d. airgun
8. A woman is most likely to be attacked:
   a. on a dark street
   b. outdoors in daylight
   c. at home
9. People most likely to be attacked in the street are:
   a. women aged 16–24
   b. men aged 16–24
   c. women aged 60 and over
   d. men aged 60 and over

10. In what percentage of recorded offences are firearms used?
    a. 0.2%
    b. 32%
    c. 7.1%
11. Between 1989 and 1990, according to recorded figures, offences of gross indecency with a child:
    a. rose by 11%
    b. fell by 17%
    c. rose by 6%
12. In a car-park it is always safest to display your parking ticket in your car windscreen. True or false?
13. To which of these age groups is a burglar most likely to belong?
    a. 14–20 years
    b. 23–26 years
14. The approximate percentage of sexual offences amongst all recorded crime is:
    a. 17%
    b. 1%
    c. 8%
15. At what age is it legal for a child to drink alcohol outside a bar or public house?
    a. 5+
    b. 8+
    c. 14+

2. Crime Risks

'A single death is a tragedy. A million deaths is a statistic.' This remark, attributed to Stalin, is highly appropriate to the way in which most people think about crime. For the rarer a crime is, the more people seem to fear it. The number of children abducted by strangers or murdered in the UK, every year, is minute, for example. Yet often parents take enormous precautions to avoid the remote possibility of these things happening to their children. Similarly it is known that women are at very low risk of attack on suburban streets. Yet in many such areas females avoid walking the pavements, even in daylight.

In both these examples there is an inverse ratio between fear and risk. The less something is likely to happen the more precautions people take to prevent it. And in the mean time commonplace risks are virtually disregarded. Parents agonize about their children being abducted while neglecting to teach them the safe way to cross a busy road. Many people are obsessed by the relatively small likelihood of street attack, but they leave their homes wide open to the much greater threat of burglary (these of course are generalizations: obviously not everybody behaves like this).

This disparity, between real and perceived danger, derives, partly from the idiosyncrasies of our psychology. The human mind focuses more easily on uncommon and extreme phenomena than on commonplace ones, as the quotation above suggests. Another factor, reinforcing this, is the mass media obsession with the 'saleability' of dramatically presented sexual and violent crime. This in turn is exploited by pressure groups and political organizations which manipulate people by working on their fears. These things lead, then, to what we might call the two Big Mistakes of our crime consciousness. Big Mistake number one is the idea that those crimes which we fear most, and which we read most about, are the crimes which most threaten us. Big Mistake number two is the notion that the crimes which obsess lobby organizations and certain politicians are, likewise, those most worthy of concern.

One aim of this book is to offer people a way out of this distortion. Our object is to discuss real risk, real crime, in pursuit of the larger goal of helping people to cope with things as they actually are. Of course it may be hard for us to view the issue as clearly as we would wish. But what we do know is that there are lots of people out there who are busy committing all sorts of crimes. Most of these crimes may be much more mundane than those we constantly hear about, but we are still entitled to reasonable protection from them. And the initial task is to find a means of judging how likely they are to affect our lives.

One way of tackling this question is to say that assessing the risk of crime is like reading a map, a map of crime. At first we look at the crime map's overall terrain, then at specific locations in the landscape. 'Location' is determined not just by where someone lives, but by other factors affecting crime risks: age, gender, type of housing, for instance. So by looking at the map as a whole, and then at specific 'places' on it, we can estimate different risks that affect different people.

Of course, a map is always just a representation. By its very nature it is not the real thing. And inevitably it is the result of a process of approximation, based on probabilities and averages. It cannot tell you exactly what will happen to you if you take a certain route, and there will be qualifications attached to even the most general information it provides. But like all maps it gives you choices. It indicates the options open to you and the obstacles that await on whatever path you choose. It puts you in the 'crime landscape' but you still have to work things out for yourself and to make decisions.

Another way of putting it is to talk about each person having a Risk Quotient (RQ). This is simply the sum of the main different crime factors affecting a certain individual. A young man in London, for instance, will have an RQ for assault which will be very different from that of a middle-aged woman in Avon and Somerset. Again, of course, the RQ cannot account for all the thousands of variations that affect people's lives. Yet it can tell people roughly where, on the crime map, they are 'starting from'. And on the basis of that information they can begin making decisions about crime and risk in their own lives.

So in the following an attempt is made, first of all, to 'map' the general incidence of crime in Britain. Then we try to locate more specific risks, within that map, by examining the risks affecting individuals. Again it must be stressed that this cannot be as precise as we would wish: we simply do not have the numbers that we need for exact calculation; and it is hard in any case to imagine a set of figures that could measure all the variables that affect crime, safety and law enforcement.

In what follows, therefore, we look first at the general risk of crime and how it has developed over the last decade. We examine the distribution of different types of crime, in their broader aspects. Then we try to concentrate our focus, to narrow things down as it were, so that we can give some idea of the crime risk for different categories of people.

GENERAL CRIME RISK

Recorded crime, in England, Scotland and Wales, has escalated remarkably over the last decade. And although the most recent figures indicate that the rate of increase might be slowing, the overall trend has been disastrous for all those concerned with law enforcement. 'Crime has simply gone through the roof and there's nothing Mr Plod can do about it,' was a typical comment. All sorts of explanations have been offered for the phenomenon, ranging from police inefficiency to the possible effects of the recession and the growth of an underclass.

However, research indicates that things may not be as alarming as they first appear. The statistical increase might partly be caused by increased reporting and recording and other technical factors, rather than by increased occurrence alone. Yet even when this is allowed for we are still left with what seem to be major crime increases, with all their attendant misery and expense.

Predictably, the bulk of this crime rise has been caused by offences far removed from those that attract most public attention.

Despite the popular impression, violent and sexual offences just do not occur very often. You are far more likely to be burgled, or to have your car stolen, than you are to be assaulted, raped or murdered. The fact that we hear so much about the latter offences does not mean that they occur more often. In 1991, for example, recorded sexual offences, of all degrees of severity, in England and Wales reached a total of 29,400 recorded crimes in a population of more than 50 million. This was below 1% of all recorded offences, in England and Wales, in that year. Violent offences recorded in 1991, in England and Wales, amounted to 190,000, about 4% of all recorded crime.

In the following pages some basic crime data are presented, to give an idea of the amount and type of crime in the country overall. This provides the right background for the consideration of more specific risks which follows. First we look at the most recent and topical statistics. Then we examine the crime rises of the last decade, from several different angles.

Most of the figures derive from Home Office and police sources. Obviously all statistical information, wherever it comes from, must be handled with care. Most of the raw numbers concern England and Wales, although Scotland is not neglected, and general trends in Scotland tend to echo those in England and Wales.

All our data, except those generated by the British Crime Survey, are ultimately based on offences recorded by the police. A large amount of crime, most of it trivial, is not brought to police attention. Thus much lesser crime is not registered in police figures (see the entry on the British Crime Survey).

Recorded Crime in 1992, in England, Wales and Scotland

Crime, as mentioned above, showed huge recorded increases throughout the 1980s. The latest available crime figures, for England and Wales in 1992, show a fall in the rate of increase. Recorded crime rose some 6% on the previous year, from 5.3 to 5.6 million offences. This is a much smaller rate of growth than the double-figure rises of the immediately preceding years. The clear-up rate dropped from 29% to 26%, continuing the decline from the 1988 clear-up rate of 35% (clear-up rates are not mentioned a great deal in this book – they are a rather ambiguous and unsatisfactory measure of police activity, largely because they are so loosely defined). Within the larger figure burglary rose 11%, sexual offences remained static and serious offences of violence rose 12% (although violent and sexual offences are still very rare). The fact that recorded crime rose 'only' by 6%, compared to the previous year, was seized upon by government ministers who were eager to claim that at last they had the apparent crime wave under control. Others said that this just showed how bad things had become: in previous periods nobody would have claimed that a 6% rise was good news.

In Scotland the annual figures for 1992 were greeted even more eagerly by those in authority. The 1992 total of recorded crime was 590,000 (rounded figures), a fall of 0.5%, after major increases in the previous few years. Burglary dropped 3%, to 113,000 offences. Violent and sexual crimes remained rare, although sexual assault rose from 1400 in 1991 to 1600 in 1992.

It is still too early to say whether these modest signs of a slow-down in crime will be sustained. In any case it would take an awful lot to reverse significantly the recorded crime increases of the last decade. And the overall crime pattern, in its incidence and spread, remains that established in the previous ten years. It is useful to examine those patterns before we go any further.

Rising Recorded Crime: 1981–1991

Crime recorded by the police rose dramatically between 1981 and 1991. When the decade commenced about 3 million crimes were recorded, at a rate of about 5.6 per 100 people. Ten years later the total had swollen to 5.3 million, or around 10 per 100 people. Most years saw increases, and the average rate of increase was about 6%, although in two years, 1983 and 1988, recorded offences actually declined. It was at the beginning of the '90s that the biggest increases came: 17% in 1990 and 16% in 1991. The vast majority of offences were 'against property'. Sexual and violent crimes were rare.

Scottish crime trends were similar. Different recording practices and legal systems make precise comparisons difficult, but the overall factors at work replicated those of England and Wales. The total of recorded crimes in Scotland rose from 481,000 in 1987 to 593,000 in 1991, for example (the figures have been rounded). In that period the rate per 100 people grew from 9.4 to 11.6.

The section of this book which deals with policing gives detailed indications of how recorded crime risks vary in different regions.

The British Crime Survey

The British Crime Survey (BCS) conducts periodic investigations into the extent and nature of crime in England and Wales. It provides some interesting perspectives on the whole process of crime and its recording in England and Wales. It is a Home Office initiative and uses survey techniques not available to the police when they record crime in normal circumstances (for further discussion of the BCS see the section on police performance).

One of the main points about the BCS is its claim that its surveys detect crime, especially less serious crime, that has not been reported to and recorded by the police.

An important contention made by the BCS, concerning crime risk assessments, is that the huge crime rises of the 1980s were heavily influenced by increased reporting. In England and Wales certain categories of recorded crime, including theft, domestic burglary, vandalism and violence against the person, considered as a group within the larger total, rose nearly 100% in the relevant decade.

The BCS suggests that about 50% of this increase was actually caused by increased reporting (more people now have telephones and need to report even small crimes to claim insurance, etc.) rather than greater occurrence. So if this is true the real crime rise between 1981 and 1991 for these important offences is half what the conventional recorded figures indicate. (The crimes the BCS figures are here compared to make up only a part of recorded crime; BCS figures are not, in this case, directly comparable with other offences, so it is not possible to extend the BCS analysis to all crime recorded.)

The BCS continues to be one of the most intriguing sources of crime information and ideas. Many people will be eager to see how it affects our perception of crime in the near future.

The BCS supplies fascinating insights into the whole crime process. But we do not have the space here to go into all its aspects (see the entry about such crime surveys in the section about policing).

Case Study: Murder Down the Ages

Has society become steadily more violent? The view that it has is challenged by historical research. An example of such work is that of Ted Robert Gurr, an American academic. According to him, 'murderous brawls and violent death were everyday occurrences' in the England of the Middle Ages. Neighbours fought with cudgels and knives. The city of Oxford, for instance, recorded 110 murders per 100,000 people in the year 1340, a phenomenal figure, way above any comparable British murder statistics in the present period (in 1989, for example, the homicide total for England and Wales was 627).

Like many other academics Gurr argues that the development of modern policing had little to do with the declining murder rate (murder rates actually rose in the 40 years following the creation of the modern British police service in 1827). After the rises of the 1980s, which the police have been able to do little about, this opinion may not surprise very many people.

PERSONAL RISK

Having examined the background threat of crime, as it were, we can now move from an assessment of the 'macro' risk to a more personal or 'micro' risk measurement for individuals.

Certain published statistics allow us to build a Risk Quotient, according to a person's age, gender and locality.

Of great value for this purpose is a table produced by the British Crime Survey. This provides the risk variation, for certain crimes, according to the neighbourhood in which people live. It judges the risk against a national average score of 100 and assumes that the crimes referred to occur in the individual's home area (this of course is not always the case with car crime or robbery/theft from the person – so there is in-built distortion in some of the figures, although they are still extremely useful).

BCS Assessment of Residential Risks

	Burglary	Autocrime around the home	Robbery/Theft from the person
A. Agricultural areas.	20	20	50
B. Modern family housing, higher income areas.	60	70	70
C. Older housing, of intermediate status.	70	100	60
D. Older terraced housing.	120	160	100

E. Better-off council estates.	90	110	120
F. Less well-off council estates.	150	160	100
G. Poorest council estates.	280	240	200
H. Mixed inner metropolitan areas.	180	190	340
I. High-status non-family areas.	220	150	250
J. Affluent suburban housing.	70	70	70
K. Better-off retirement areas.	70	80	70
Indexed national average.	100	100	100

To this we can add our own measurements, based on age, gender and region; in the case of theft of cars we can also 'count in' the type of car at risk, given that some makes of car are stolen far more often than others. We should look at each factor in turn before making some calculations.

Region: We can give a score for crime per 100 people in each area of England and Wales (see the table on p. 222).

(see the table on p. 222)

12 plus crimes=60
9–12=50
7–9=40
5–7=30
4–5=20
less than 4=10

Age, which is a factor in Robbery/Theft from the person, scores as follows:

male 16–30=40
female 19–35=25

These are the high-risk ages for such crime, and for simplicity we can discount other age groups.

Gender, also relevant, scores as follows:

male=60
female=40

The age and gender weighting reflect the fact that young men are the main victims.

Car type: Theft risk assessments are based on the tables on pp. 203–6).

high risk=60
medium risk=30
low risk=10

We can make all sorts of deductions from these criteria. A family resident in 'Modern family housing in a higher income area' would have a burglary risk factor of 60, which is 40% below the national average of 100. If the region were Devon and Cornwall, where crime per 100 population is 7 to 9, then there is an added risk factor of 40, providing a total burglary Risk Quotient of 100.

This is much lower than the risk run by a family on a council estate in Redcar. Their neighbourhood is categorized as 'Poorest council estates', with a risk score of 280, nearly three times the national average. Cleveland is in the highest per capita crime category, of 12 plus crimes per 100 population, giving a risk score of 60 and a total burglary Risk Quotient of 340, nearly three and a half times higher than that for the family in Devon and Cornwall (in addition, the exact type of house could be added to the figures: end-of-terrace houses carry higher risks, for example – but for present purposes this is over-complex).

For car crime the figures can be computed in a similar style. Somebody in Thames Valley, living in 'Older housing of intermediate status' and owning a BMW 700 Series (E32), would have a low Risk Quotient for theft of their car, totalling 180; this is much less than the 270 scored by someone living in 'A high-status non-family area' in London, and in possession (perhaps temporarily . . .) of a Ford Capri Mk2.

Again a 28-year-old man, residing in a neighbourhood classed among the 'Poorest council estates', in Northumbria, is at much higher street crime risk than a 45-year-old woman who lives in the same sort of neighbourhood in adjoining Durham. His age and gender count against him, as does the fact that Northumbria has a higher per capita crime rate than Durham. His Risk Quotient for street crime is 360, compared to her 290.

To a large extent, using such figures in this manner is a sort of game. It resembles a game because, like most statistics, it simplifies complex things. And the 'cold numbers' themselves omit many of the variables that affect both human behaviour and the laws of chance. And of course the weighting given to different factors can be fairly arbitrary.

Nonetheless it is a game worth playing. It encourages us to start thinking about what our own crime risks might be. Thinking about crime, rather than just reacting to it, is an important part of learning to cope with its significance in our lives. Using the figures provided above, you can work out your own crime risks, and those of people you know, or of people like you who might live in different housing and/or parts of the country.

Having read this section readers should now be able to think more accurately about their own risk levels. This will help in making use of other parts of the book. For instance, someone at high risk of burglary should pay close attention to the section on home security. They may also wish to install more home security devices than someone whose burglary Risk Quotient is quite low.

CONCLUSIONS

In concluding this section of the book certain fundamental points deserve emphasis.

1. Most crimes are committed against property, not against people.

2. Sexual and violent offences compose only a fraction of all crimes.

3. Those who think they are most at risk are often those least at risk. Women and the elderly face a much lower threat of street crime than young men, for instance. In fact the figures reveal that men are twice as likely as women to become street assault victims across all age groups. Men's greater physical strength does not make them much safer. Assailants will ensure they are physically stronger, or will have superior numbers, or will use weapons.

4. Most rapes involve people known to each other and they occur indoors. The most likely victims are aged between 16 and 24. Those least at risk of rape are under the age of 10 and over 60. Male rapes are increasingly reported, although these also are rare.

British Standards

In an attempt to improve the quality of alarms, and other security fitments, the British Standards Institution has begun to prepare appropriate specifications. Look for evidence that purchased systems follow British Standards requirements. For house alarm installations the British Standard is 4737, and you should get written confirmation that alarms have been installed to its specifications. Door locks should conform to BS 3621. Look for the British Standards kite mark on the product. The British Standard for wire-free alarms is BS 6799. For DIY alarms it is BS 6707.

For car alarms the standard is BS 6803.

For car locks and general car security it is BS AU 209.

Contact the British Standards Institution for full details.

See contact details in the Reference Section.

3. Personal Safety

No area of crime and crime prevention, as we have seen in the previous chapter, is as open to misinterpretation as that of personal safety. The wilful and spiteful distortion of statistics in this field is outrageous. It is important to remind people, therefore, that street assaults, rape, child abduction and domestic violence are all rare occurrences.

Nonetheless, although such incidents are rare, they are extremely traumatic when they do occur. The injuries and shock suffered are severe enough. But these are made even worse by the fear of repetition. A single attack can alter a person's way of life for ever, simply by making them so frightened of certain places or types of people that they avoid environments that many of us would regard as innocuous. Someone attacked on a crowded railway station platform may long afterwards find it difficult to get on a train or a bus, for instance. A woman who had been raped ten years before said: 'It happened very early one morning . . . in broad daylight . . . on my way to work . . . He pulled me into a doorway in a side street . . . I made a lot of noise but although people must have heard no one paid any attention. A week later I took my first driving lesson. Now I never walk anywhere . . .'

Men also experience what one of them bitterly termed the 'horizon-shrinking effects' of fear, and they suffer them more often than women, as, outside the home, they are violently attacked far more frequently. Men have additional problems: women as well as men expect them to 'perform': to show courage and resource when under threat. 'It really gets to me,' one man said. 'Sometimes I've been in an awkward situation and I just wanted to run, to cut out. Get away from it. But I couldn't. I had to make some sort of a go of it. People despise a bloke if they see him back off unless it's against overwhelming force. A woman could burst into tears and nobody would think the worse of her and if she stood up for herself people would be full of praise. But a bloke is expected to handle things anyway, as a matter of routine, and nobody shows any particular interest.'

Many men who have been assaulted feel that they received less help from the appropriate agencies than others. Most adult males intensely dislike being labelled as 'victims'. They are relatively self-reliant and uncomfortable with the operational style used by conventional victim support groups. This does not, however, mean that they have no feelings and no need of help.

Yet, however differently the genders are treated after they have been targeted by criminals, one thing is the same for both genders and all ages: few people *want* to be a victim. Although the likelihood of attack is much lower than lurid headlines or heavily slanted 'research' suggest, it is still worth taking precautions.

It is important therefore that individuals learn how to look after themselves. Looking after yourself is not simply a question of procedures, of learning the tricks of the self-protection trade, as it were. It is also about attitude, about your overall approach, and about your knowledge of how public debate over these matters is developing. Accordingly we examine appropriate social and cultural issues, and such questions as awareness, manner, and methods of dealing with aggressors. We also look at self-protection in different environments, and we consider the implications for different social groups.

The Public

The general public continues to hold a distorted view of what police call 'crimes against the person'. Many people barricade themselves into their houses at night, despite the extremely low risk of attack. In the popular imagination the world beyond the front door is a place of confrontation and threat, involving rapes, sexual assaults and child abduction.

Much of the blame for this exaggerated fear must be taken by sectors of the media and by certain pressure groups. The former want to sell news stories by sensationalizing them. They are also often obsessed by particular social problems and issues which are crime-related, and the obsession influences their judgement. The latter want to gain grants and influence by exaggerating the threat to the victims whom they claim to represent. Police and politicians, too, are capable of exploiting public fear of crime when it is convenient.

The excessive fear of assault, particularly street assault and mugging, severely damages social and community life. Pedestrianism and casual neighbourhood contact have, for instance, declined dramatically. People drive everywhere instead of walking as they once did.

The irony is that the fear-induced decline of pedestrianism actually adds to the low risk that does exist. On the streets there are fewer people around to help when things go wrong. Muggers and vandals are encouraged by the prospect of preying on those who are alone on otherwise empty pavements. The loss of general neighbourliness, of simple friendliness, is another consequence of this state of affairs.

There are no immediate signs that things are about to change. Pressure groups, media organizations and other interested parties have too much to gain from emphasizing and exaggerating the threat of such crimes.

The Criminals

Defining the perpetrators of crimes against the person is not a simple business. These crimes cover such a wide span of human activity that there is no single group of offenders. For instance, many offences of violence and sexual assault, including rape, are committed indoors by people known to the victim. Domestic offenders spread across all the categories of age, occupation and gender. A majority of offences seem to be committed by males, although female-perpetrated assaults and sexual offences are by no means unknown (they may be reported less, and may be taken less seriously by the police).

Those committing street assault and mugging, however, tend to be overwhelmingly youthful and male, although there are a few exceptions to this rule. They are less likely than domestic assailants to know their victims beforehand, and many of them come from the impoverished parts of our society.

Trends over the past decade have generally made things much harder for those committing these offences indoors. Such crimes have been pursued with enhanced vigour by the police and associated agencies, especially those associated with child abuse and casual violence towards women. This emphasis is likely to continue for some time, despite concern in some quarters that the pursuit is over-zealous and heavy-handed, particularly with regard to child abuse.

Simultaneously those committing street offences have found life comparatively easier. Confusion over sentencing policy, plus a desire to reduce the prison population, have made it less likely that these offenders will be jailed (the police have been especially annoyed by what they regard as the deficiencies, in this respect, of the Criminal Justice Act). The sheer pressure and complexity of demands on police resources also make it harder to combat street assaults and harassment.

It will be interesting to see if the planned changes to the police and criminal justice systems (see the chapter on policing) have an effect. If they result in a more consistent sentencing policy, plus the presence of significantly more police on the beat, then street criminals may be placed under greater pressure.

The Police

A feature of the last few years has been the major police response to sexual and racial crimes and domestic violence. Most forces have set up special units or other facilities to deal with these offences, devoting much time, energy and money to considering how service can be improved. Special interview suites have been

built; officers have been trained in both investigative and counselling techniques.

This shows the extent, contrary to popular belief, to which
police respond to pressure groups and lobbyists. Campaign
groups are extremely active in this field, dealing with all sorts
of victims, from battered women to male victims of rape. Some
feel the police are a little too responsive to such issues. It is
argued that these crimes are comparatively rare, and that the
emphasis on them is not justified. Others say that the obsession
with domestic violence units and so on is a form of displacement,
a way of diverting attention from the comparative failure of the
police to cope with other forms of crime against the person,
especially street assault and public disorder.

The extraordinary muddle and inconsistency which typify
contemporary government and administration in this country
make prediction difficult. Nonetheless, the prevailing ethos,
within the Home Office and the Inspectorate of Constabulary,
probably signifies that the emphasis on combating problems
associated with gender, race and domestic violence will persist.
The huge media interest in these issues reinforces this. Budgetary
restraints may, though, to some extent restrain further development of police activity in this area.

A fascinating but ever more complex question, which we have
already raised, is this: will the impending reorganization of the
law enforcement structure put more police on street patrol? This
goal is currently shared by all parts of the mainstream political
world, including those on the left who were formerly distrustful
of most types of police activity. Fear of public disorder and
street attack is widespread and the demand for a more 'visible
policing' style is popular. But previous attempts to get police
out of their enclaves and on to patrol have been fragmentary
and unconvincing. Much of the blame for this should be taken
by the government and the Civil Service for loading police
officers with responsibilities that make it hard for them to escape
from the office. Will things change in this respect? An open
question.

The Government

The Home Office is the agency chiefly responsible for giving flesh to the government's thoughts about crime and personal safety. This, in practice, causes dreadful problems. For the internal Home Office philosophy is dominated, especially regarding crimes against the person, by the sort of liberal criminology that is despised by Tory apparatchiks. The Conservative penchant, at least in theory, for Sturdy Self-Reliance blends very uneasily indeed with the Home Office Victim Culture.

Yet despite such differences both these Key Players in the crime world are stuck with each other. No matter how long it stays in control the Conservative government seems incapable of altering the world view of those in charge at Queen Anne's Gate. And the Civil Service has no power, at least directly, to remove governments, however much some of its members may wish to do so.

The result, for the public, and for the law enforcement system generally, is disastrous. The two contradictory approaches are handcuffed together by the demands of our constitution. Yet each inclines in a different direction, each cancels out the other's best gambits, as it were. The eventual outcome is a dreary compromise. Home Office ministers call for tougher punishment of offenders; at the same time many of their Civil Servants analyse crime in a manner which steers away from discussions of personal responsibility.

The political opposition, especially the Labour Party, has taken advantage of the feebleness caused by this split consciousness. Its representatives have learnt to combine, rather than be confused by, the two different penological traditions. They have appropriated some of the Lash Them and Lock Them rhetoric that once was heard only at Conservative Party conferences, skilfully blending this sort of talk with the left's customary emphasis on social and economic deprivation as a cause of criminality.

In practice, this development probably makes little difference. The opposition may have to wait a long time before it gets the chance to take office, and it is one thing to blend such different traditions on paper; it is another matter, however carefully you have planned it, to fuse them in the world of action, even if Labour were eventually re-elected into government. The left, in the end, may be just as compromised by contradictory viewpoints as is the right. Unless something changes dramatically the country is lumbered, for the foreseeable future, with a policy-making apparatus, in the arena of crime and personal safety, that is inherently paradoxical.

Industry and Commerce

There exists a considerable, but rather shapeless and incoherent, market for personal safety devices, including personal alarms and other protective mechanisms. To an extent the industry supplying this market is checked by legal controls. These aim to make it hard for companies or individuals to cross the border separating protective technology from offensive weapons.

Estimating how this technology will evolve is difficult. The basic legal limitations restrict innovation, and some of the more ingenious devices, such as paint sprays and smell sprays, can be turned against those they should protect. Nor have we yet reached the stage where obvious, if slightly risible, market developments are explored: very few people seem to be buying or supplying simple body armour, to be worn under clothing, for instance.

Industry and commerce are also enmeshed in personal safety issues through the establishment, promotion and dissemination of training programmes. Sometimes these services are 'bought in' by major companies; on a smaller level members of the public enter directly into this kind of training, often on a purely local basis.

Overall encouragement is given, by government and its agencies, to companies interested in sponsoring appropriate crime prevention. Crime Concern is one quango which, with mixed success, has sought private backing for such initiatives.

It is hard to get an overview of the matter as a whole. Industry and commerce, by their nature, are increasingly decentralized and diffuse in the range of their activities. What is likely, given the government's free-market tastes, is that industry and commerce will increasingly influence crime prevention styles in this area. The government wants to 'privatize' as much crime prevention and policy as possible. Whether this is beneficial or disastrous it will, initially, be extremely confusing. Private companies do not combine easily with public sector organizations like the police and the Civil Service.

The Media

Which is the group whose activities and opinions make the biggest impact on public policy, concerning crime against the person? It is not the perpetrators of these offences. Nor is it the victims. It is in fact journalists. Reporters and feature writers and news editors largely determine how such crime, indeed all crime, is perceived both by the public and by the authorities.

Sometimes the results are ludicrous. Media priorities differ markedly from those of other parts of society. And professionals operating in the small, surprisingly closed world of journalism can be just as prone to preconception and selective use of evidence as members of any other group. Even reputable writers, on 'good' newspapers, are pressurized into emphasizing the dramatic aspects of the events they report. One consequence of this is a distorted public awareness of criminal threat. Women, for instance, despite all the evidence indicating that the main victims of assault are male, are encouraged to feel at constant risk of attack. Child abduction, an extremely rare occurrence, is given such enormous publicity that community life is severely damaged by the fear and over-vigilance that the intense coverage inspires.

The media have a powerful role in influencing government thinking on crime and safety, however much some politicians may claim to despise the popular press. Politicians are often too busy for personal reflection, and get many of their basic ideas from TV, radio and newspapers. They also need to show awareness of and responsiveness to the worries of the electorate. These worries, in the field of crime and personal safety, are very much determined by what journalists decide to write about. And the influence of newspapers, TV and radio will increase as the world becomes media-saturated.

This media control has benefits as well as disadvantages. A number of journalists are relentless in their pursuit of official malpractice. One result has been the exposure of a great deal of corruption, at all levels of the criminal justice system.

The problem for the public, especially regarding something as vital as crime and personal safety, is that the media world is not necessarily a replica of the real world. Journalists live in small, professional communities under constant pressure. Like other such groups they can easily develop a collective psychology that distances them from the very facts they are supposed to report. They can impose their own obsessions on events, disregarding evidence that does not fit their pre-formed viewpoints. And increasingly work pressures mean that they find it hard to escape from the office for any significant length of time. They themselves often rely on second-hand sources: statistics cooked by less than impartial lobbyists, reports hastily thrown together by press agencies, and so on. Even correspondents on the ground are at the mercy of news managers and press officers. These individuals carefully doctor information before it becomes available to the media.

There is a real danger, in such circumstances, that journalists will respond even more to their own personal obsessions and internal data sources and even less to the actuality of life on the street. In response the media audience has to exert great care in assessing what it is told, especially over such volatile topics as crime and assault.

Perhaps journalists should look sceptically at some of their working methods. Members of the public, likewise, would benefit from the right kind of media education at school and college. This should not be covert liberal studies, but a hard-nosed analysis of how news and views are generated and collected. Without such attempts at counterbalance the press will

continue to distort our understanding of crime and personal
safety.

Research

A large amount of criminological research directly or indirectly
concerns personal safety. Universities, voluntary organizations
and pressure groups like Victim Support, NACRO and the Suzy
Lamplugh Trust, the Home Office, the police themselves: these
are all amongst the bodies which sponsor and/or engage directly
in this sort of research.

Much of the work undertaken is about children, ethnic min-
orities and women. Obviously it is important to examine the
needs of these groups. Yet the problems of assault faced by
white men, who make up many of the victims, are largely
ignored. Some critics complain about this. Others say also that
a lot of current research is too ideological, and is concerned
more with furthering certain social objectives than with finding
out the truth about crime and victimization. Whatever the merits
of the matter it is possible that at some stage there will be a
debate about this, along the lines of other debates, in other
areas, about race and gender. Yet for the moment the minorities-
plus-women-and-children focus dominates research priorities.

There is also a certain amount of current investigation into
the practicalities of crime prevention schemes and other safety
projects and stratagems. Much academic research has a strong
influence on journalists and on police and government policy.
A lot of it, also, is of a fairly obscure and theoretical type and
makes little impact outside the academy.

Predicting the activities of the present government, in this
arena, is a perilous business. But it is likely that researchers
will be affected by the general pressures that policy-makers are
exerting on the academic community. Those active in the field
will be encouraged to seek commercial links and to develop
entrepreneurial styles. There may gradually be greater stress on
applied research, in the field of crime against the person, and

less on the more abstract questions. Institutions may be encouraged to ensure that research results are disseminated as widely as possible. These changes, if they are carried through, may simply lead to confusion: the market obsessions of the current government do not necessarily blend well with the outlook and methods of researchers active in this area. On the other hand, if researchers are inspired towards work which is of greater practical benefit to the populace in general, without loss of academic integrity, everybody may benefit.

SELF-PROTECTION: TECHNIQUES AND STRATAGEMS

Case Study: Street Incident
by Glen Warren

Tony decided to take the short cut. He walked fast, head down, hands in pockets. There were no lights in the street – they'd all been smashed by hooligans, Tony decided. The only illumination came from the odd kitchen window in the houses. He hesitated, then went on: he was just fifty yards from the pub, and bloody freezing. He thought he heard a noise and quickened his pace. He strained his ears but now he could hear nothing; must have been imagining things, he decided.

Two arms clamped around his chest, pinning his own arms tight against his sides. His heart seemed to throw itself, with terrible slowness, across his torso.

'Hand it over, you bastard. Hand it over.' A youth appeared in front of him, the bottom half of his face covered by a scarf. Tony struggled against the arms constraining him, his heart pulsing faster and faster.

'Come on, hand it over.' The youth leaned closer, his arm jerking forward. A wave of pain buckled Tony's stomach. He still struggled. More blows came. Now pain raided his arms, legs, sides. Suddenly the arms holding him loosened; he hit the ground, his mind dazed.

He felt hands scurrying through his pockets. 'Look at this,' said another voice, deeper than the first. Tony forced open his eyes. He saw a tall youth holding up his wrist-watch. Instinctively he half rose on one elbow, his hand reaching. Pain once more dashed itself against his head. Something propelled him to the ground.

'Stay down. Stay down, you bastard.'

Tony felt his stomach heaving, the warm trickle of blood from his nose. A car door slammed somewhere not too far away.

'Come on. Fuck it. Come on.' It was the deeper voice again, only now the words came faster.

Tony felt the vomit rise into his mouth, struggled to his knees, half fearing another blow. At that moment he heard the desperate scurry of footsteps, a voice rising into the air from the direction of the pub. He opened his eyes. The youths had gone. A man he vaguely recognized was running towards him. Only now, his face covered in blood, did he have time to feel the anger and shame pressing up inside him.

Aggressive Encounters: the Reality

When real violence breaks out it can be very different from what people expect. Their major experiences of it may be second-hand. Everybody who has a television will have seen countless dramatized killings and acts of mayhem. If they have encountered actual violence it may have been a long time before. In memory the event is more coherent than it was when it happened: we tend to edit our recollections, to forget the bits that do not fit, just as a TV film editor will tidy up the footage from a fight scene.

What surprises people, given this background, is the shapelessness of many violent incidents. They are messy and result from miscalculation rather than design. Not many individuals, including those who are heavily disturbed or under the influence of drink or drugs, actually want to engage in a real fight: even when the odds favour you it is a risky business. Most fights are like car crashes. Often the aggressor, like a speeding driver who

goes that bit too fast, has simply misjudged the degree of bullying that his victim will passively take. There is usually a great
deal of noise. The participants scream and shout; they repeat
themselves incoherently. When they deliver blows they do so in
sudden, jerky flurries. The action is uneven. It stops and starts
and it is hard to know when it is finally over. And the results
are normally mundane: the winning side is the one which gets
the first blow in and is superior in numbers or physical strength.

What the onlookers see, then, usually has none of the coher-
ence and decisiveness that characterize violence on film or the
stage. What the victim feels, apart from physical pain, is shock
and confusion: everything happened so quickly, and there was
no time to think. And no amount of theory or gym practice can
prepare someone for what it feels like when a fist, or a blade,
is driven hard and repeatedly into the face.

These things should be remembered when considering self-
protection techniques and stratagems.

Knowing Yourself

Perhaps the one most vital subject for study, in protecting yourself, is your own psychology. We do not have the space, in this
book, to investigate the intricacies of the human personality.
Nonetheless it is possible to indicate the sort of questions you
should ask yourself about your own behaviour. A little self-
analysis, in conjunction with the practical advice offered in our
text, will help you to understand your own safety requirements.
For you must build your safety strategy around your own needs.
Knowing certain things about yourself will help you to assess
your chances. Maybe you will find that there are certain aspects
of your behaviour that you need to restrain because they are
reckless or needlessly provocative. Or you might decide that in
some ways you are not sufficiently assertive, that you give off
the 'victim' vibes that attract trouble as much as undue aggression. What sort of person, then, are you?

1. Are you easily upset by the casual comments of strangers or acquaintances?

2. Are you quick-tempered?

3. Are you excessively concerned about losing face in public?

4. Or alternatively, are you too pliable, too easily pushed around?

5. Do you give the impression that you would provide absolutely no resistance to assaults upon you?

6. Are you observant and well organized, and likely to spot trouble before it spots you?

7. Or are you the sort of individual who is rarely aware of what goes on around them?

8. Do you plan your movements when you go out for the evening?

9. Or do you operate on an entirely spontaneous basis?

10. Do you know how you would instinctively respond if without warning you were exposed to threat?

11. How long would it take you to get over the shock of a minor assault?

These are just some of the questions you could ask yourself. The central point is not that of asking any particular question but the value, within certain limits, of practical self-analysis. The emphasis should be on balance, on working out whether you might over- or under-react to threat and violence. What you need is to be able to respond to such problems in a controlled yet decisive manner. You need to be conciliatory without being soft, decisive and well organized without being aggressive. Each individual must work out the balance for themselves, in their own lives, in view of their own tastes and habits. But you begin by asking: what sort of person am I?

Awareness

Much of modern life is designed to prevent close encounters with strangers, or for that matter with any kind of unpredictable phenomena. We put mechanical objects between ourselves and the outside world; we use them as protective devices: televisions and telephones, radios, fax machines. We drive everywhere. All these things allow us to distance ourselves from our chaotic and bewildering society.

It is good for us that we can do this. But there is a problem. Our insulated habits mean that we are less skilled in dealing with unstable and aggressive people or environments than our ancestors were. When somebody nearby does something shocking we perhaps react more slowly than they did, and with a sense of disbelief. We spend so much time viewing life through a screen that it is hard to believe it is really happening

We need to relearn certain skills. Sometimes we will be alone on the street or indoors in proximity to highly excitable individuals. We need to be aware of what is going on around us, so that we are neither immobilized by fear, nor taken wildly by surprise, when things go wrong.

So it is necessary to cultivate an awareness, a capacity to 'read' people and places. For areas, like people, have particular characteristics. Some parts of them are less attractive than others. They behave differently at different times. Sometimes they resemble each other from a distance, but the resemblance vanishes when you see them close up, just like people.

Those who wish to avoid attack must, then, give some thought to where and when, and from whom, they will be most at risk. They must also study their own strengths, weaknesses, and mood variations. Observance of the following points helps to build the best sort of instinctive safety awareness.

1. Planning

When you are going somewhere think ahead. Obviously the
longer the journey the more important this is. The specific
environment involved is also important: a short stroll in an inner
city locality may well demand greater caution than a lengthy
walk in a suburb. Assess the different localities you will pass
through. How rich or poor are they? Will there be lots of
unemployed youths on the streets? How much care do you need
to take? Is it important to let someone know where you are
going and when you will arrive? Will you spend much time
alone in isolated places?.

2. Borderlands

Modern cities are deceptive. The division between quiet and
disruptive areas is rarely clearly marked and is highly fluid.
You can walk fifty yards and everything changes: the rules of
behaviour change, people change, the risks change. You can
wander into some awkward encounters in this manner, with
your defences down. So be alert; this even applies in areas you
think you know well, for their social composition can alter dramatically in a year or two. Note signs of decay: street litter,
noise, stray dogs, sullen youths on street corners . . .

3. The Schizoid Locality

Another problem with many areas is that they lead separate
lives at separate times. During the day they are lively but pleasant. People of all types and ages go in and out of the shops and
cafés. At night these districts go into Vampire Mode: different,
more aggressive people are on the street, perhaps youths from
nearby housing estates. Small children, middle-aged couples and
the elderly have vanished. Those used to such places during the
day can be unpleasantly surprised if they are not ready for them
at night. The same applies to restaurants and pubs. The bar
which welcomes pensioners at midday might be packed with
very different individuals after dark. It is a good idea to remember this sort of variation when going out for the evening.

4. Foreign Parts

There has been much recent publicity about attacks on British tourists in places like Florida. Such localities can be a lot more violent than Britain. Firearms, for example, are widely carried in cities such as Miami. The consequences of getting things wrong in environments of that kind can be fatal.

When abroad it is even more important than usual to plan your journeys. Be especially aware of the differences between areas in particular towns. Do not offer any sustained resistance to someone who has a firearm. Get advice from embassies and tourist authorities, as early as you can. Be conscious, as much as possible, of differences in social customs and mannerisms.

Manner

'Manner', in this context, is really a question of self-presentation. Potential aggressors, especially when they are strangers, assess their chances on the basis of appearances. The way you carry yourself and the sort of 'presence' that you project give essential indications about what people can expect from you. Such things are particularly important in connection with street attacks, although they also have some bearing upon domestic violence.

1. Avoiding Trouble

a. The biggest problems occur when you are alone. Most street attackers are not distinguished by their courage. Very few fights, outside a boxing ring, take place between equal numbers of equally matched individuals. Assailants will usually pick on people who seem smaller and, or weaker than themselves, and often they will reduce the risk even further by making sure they are superior in numbers to any potential victims. Obviously this is not always the case. Those inspired by drugs, drink or the need to act out various obsessions will not necessarily be rational judges of the odds.

Generally speaking, the risk is much less for those in a group. But even those in groups, especially in rough areas, should exercise discretion.

b. A calm and self-confident street-demeanour deters attackers. Look confident and walk purposefully. You are much less likely to be assaulted if you do not seem vulnerable. And if your bearing is controlled but relaxed you are less likely, on the whole, to do something which, however unintentionally, provokes the sort of touchy individuals who are increasingly found on our streets.

c. Here planning and punctuality are vital, as recommended above. If you are late, tense and in a hurry, your movements will be jerky and uncoordinated. Your facial expressions will be irritable and erratic. You will look awkward, disorganized and a soft target. The same unhealthy effect will be achieved if you wander along, bumping into lamp-posts, only half conscious of your surroundings.

d. Watch how carefully people behave towards each other in violent inner city areas. At first everything seems haphazard. Yet prolonged scrutiny reveals that individuals display a low-key, indirect watchfulness. There is a kind of laconic wariness to people's movements. And you will notice that young men, unless they know each other, exchange sidelong rather than direct glances.

e. Learn from this. Do not make unsolicited eye contact with anyone you are unsure of, especially young males who may view this as a challenge or as a sign that you lack 'respect'. Look towards people, not away from them, but do not 'lock into' their gaze.

f. Walk briskly, as suggested above, but not too fast. Rapid walking attracts attention. In high-crime localities it may also suggest the tension displayed by a soft target, or it may be seen as the domineering arrogance of an interloper: the view taken by some locals will be that you are on their territory, and they will want to see acknowledgement of that in your bearing.

g. If your normal walking pace is fast it is best to slow down when you near people who look as though they might be trouble. Instead, spread your weight as you walk. This suggests solidity: someone literally in touch with the basics, someone who 'knows the score'. Additionally, it makes it easier to keep your balance if you are attacked.

h. Clothing is significant. A smartly dressed woman, in a tight mini skirt, will stand out in a run-down area and attract the attention of young males. Prosperous-looking men in suits, in poor neighbourhoods where nobody wears a suit, attract both attention and resentment. It is your right, of course, to dress as you like, but those who present a threat on the street are not deeply interested in other people's rights. If possible modify your dress style accordingly.

2. Stopping Trouble

Self-presentation has a role, then, in preventing problems. The manner a person adopts is also significant once trouble has actually begun. Sometimes you may walk into an incident which has already started, or you will encounter someone who is absolutely determined on aggression, no matter what preventive techniques are deployed.

a. Tone of voice is important. A low-pitched, measured speaking voice helps to calm things down. When you get tense your voice rises, although it rarely disappears completely. To counteract this you should sigh deeply, to release the chest muscles. This allows you to breathe in deeply. Then keep your voice low and speak slowly.

b. Stand sideways on, feet well apart for balance, and if the other person is sitting take a few steps backwards or crouch down on to their level.

c. Do not jab a finger. Do not gesticulate. An open hand gives a 'non-aggressive' signal.

d. Do not crowd the other person. Crowding someone pressures them. We all have a bodily Buffer Zone which enlarges when we feel vulnerable in any way. Keep 12 to 15 inches from them at first. Come closer as they calm down. Do not stand too far from them either, as this makes it impossible to establish a rapport.

e. Angle your head down, just a little. This is less threatening and more sympathetic. It also lets you watch their facial expressions, whilst simultaneously remaining aware of what is going on around you and of what they are doing with their hands.

f. Do not stare into their eyes. Make regular but fleeting eye contact and prolong the eye contact, bit by bit, as soon as you establish some kind of understanding.

g. When you talk, use the 'echo' technique. This reassures them that you are listening, by playing their message back to them, as it were. For example: 'I realize what you are saying . . . I know he's annoyed you . . .' etc. On to this you can tag your own message, for example: 'I know he's annoyed you, but I'm sure you've already made your point to him in return and that he won't do it again . . .'

h. Aggressive people, especially when they are young, are often very insecure and frightened of losing face (this may indeed cause some of their aggression, although it does not of course excuse it). Do nothing that might gratuitously insult them, especially in front of their peers. If they are not actually being physically violent, and if you feel in control, get them as far away as you can from the audience, without jeopardizing your own safety, even if it is just into a corner where some other people can still see you (you will want to stay within reach of witnesses). Sometimes it is amazing how quickly people calm down when they are no longer on stage before a crowd of bystanders. But remember, do not isolate yourself with someone who is still at a peak of anger. The whole idea is to get them away from the audience when they have calmed down enough to be rational, in the hope that you can talk them away from the possibility of immediately restarting the cycle of confrontation and aggression.

i. Concentrate on the person or persons most concerned. Do not yourself make the mistake of playing to the audience. Doing so may well distort your own reactions and can make little practical difference in any case: few people will want to get immediately involved. It is useless being bitter about this. Somebody may well dial 999, and occasionally bystanders will intervene, and many of them will give evidence to the police, but generally at vital moments you will find that you are on your own. This is why it is so important to get things right. Nobody will do it for you.

Physical Self-Protection

There may come a point when all these stratagems have failed; violence becomes unavoidable. Its onset will, as described above, be disorientating for almost anybody subjected to it: no matter how fit, young, experienced or courageous they may be.

1. It is in the first few seconds, when the shock and confusion are greatest, that the victim is most likely to lose control. However, there are certain physical indicators which help to warn you that somebody might be about to attack. Spotting them for what they are can give you that extra bit of time which might be crucial. Some of these indicators are quite obvious, others less so, but either way it is useful to tabulate them:

a. Clenched fists, general muscle tension in hands, limbs, face.
b. Speech which is fast and loud, or fast and high-pitched; a raised jabbing finger.

c. Jerky movements of the hands and feet.

d. An attempt to enter your 'private space', to crowd you by moving in very close.

e. Facial paleness: this means that the body is in an advanced state of readiness, on the point of vigorous physical activity of the 'fight or flight' variety. A pale face is in fact more ominous than a red face. A red-faced person will make lots of noise, but is not as threatening as an individual whose skin is drained of colour. Obviously there are exceptions to this, and of course red faces can rapidly and dramatically lose their colour . . .

2. Your first thought should always be to get away. When danger is imminent assess potential escape routes, and places where help might be obtained. Ensure the route to the door or ground-floor window is not blocked by your attacker.

3. Avoid restricted spaces, places where weapons are available, such as kitchens. Keep away from the top of staircases.

4. Physical restraint is difficult and to be avoided unless absolutely essential. Angry people can have surprising strength and can be ruthless about using weapons.

5. Self-defence is not a simple matter. Training for it needs dedication. It involves lots of time and considerable expense. Techniques must be constantly practised if they are to be of any use. Fitness must be maintained. Self-defence cannot be learnt from a book and needs regular consultation with an instructor.

6. There is also the problem of quality of life. If you spend lots of time rehearsing the art of physically immobilizing people the experience may depress you: unless you are very insensitive, or deeply fascinated by the techniques in themselves, you will find it a gloomy pursuit. Alternatively it may make you trigger-happy or over-confident and more likely to cause trouble than stop it.

7. Legs and feet: kneeing people in the groin, which is often suggested as a self-defence tactic, is not as easy as it looks when

people do it in films. It requires a fair amount of co-ordination, and men instinctively withdraw their testicles when threatened, so that they are too high up to be easily attacked. Attempts to kick out at a shin or an ankle can put you seriously off balance and can work in the attacker's favour.

8. The eyes: people frequently have the idea, gathered from self-defence manuals and videos, that they should jab fingers, pens, keys, etc. into the attacker's eyes. In practice this is far from easy. The vast majority of people will instinctively find it hard to do. As soon as you gaze into someone's eyes you form a sense of them as a personality. It therefore becomes harder to hurt them, to treat them as a 'target'. The same applies to attempts to put fingers up someone's nostrils. By extending your hand in this way you are also presenting your opponent with something he can grasp and use as a lever against you.

9. Using bags and handbags: sometimes people think that deploying bags or handbags as weapons will get them out of trouble. Only heavy bags are likely to make an impact. Yet their weight makes them unwieldy. Muggers will probably be pleased that you are giving them a chance to get hold of your property. Do not forget, either, that the weight of the bag can be turned against you. It may also make it difficult to keep your balance. And by swinging the bag you might simultaneously be presenting your assailant with both the booty and a weapon with which to subdue you. It is also worth noting the authoritative words of Diana Lamplugh 'If you hold on to your bag and have the strap around your body you are likely to be dragged along. It is better to keep some money elsewhere on your person and not to fill your bag or briefcase with so many valuable things that you cannot let it go.'

10. Keyrings: these, wrapped between the fingers, could be used when delivering a punch. Beware of the risk, however, that an assailant may get hold of them. And if this is your primary thought you could, also, lose a valuable opportunity to escape.

You must be realistic about self-protection. Many of the most commonly advised stratagems are harder to apply than they seem, as discussed above.

If you have a choice it is best to avoid trouble as much as possible. This does not mean that you should let people intimidate you. It is simply better to solve problems non-violently.

Yet things may reach a point at which you are trapped. Fighting, as hard as you can, might be your only chance of avoiding serious injury. If so, you must hold nothing back: in a fight, as opposed to a sporting event, there are no controlled victories. To avoid injury you must be ruthless.

1. Noise is a powerful weapon. Expel your breath sharply, drop your lower jaw and you will be able to shout or scream into the face of your assailant. This helps to build up a rush of adrenalin and to release latent, self-protective anger. It will also help to disorientate your opponent.

2. Spit in his face, or throw any fluids within reach into his eyes. Push your forefingers under his cheekbones. Slap both sides of his head simultaneously. Hit him hard and sharp between the eyes (this can knock him out). Twist his ears.

3. Bend the fingers back as far as they will go, pull them violently apart, stamp on them. The pain of a broken finger is excruciating and takes all your opponent's attention.

4. Aim your punches and kicks towards the centre of your attacker's body. Your limbs should move in short, stabbing motions. Most people, when they fight, use the Windmill Approach. Arms and legs flail hopelessly at the target. Great looping punches land haphazardly. Wild attempts at kicking merely cause the kicker to lose his balance. This is the wrong way. Short, concentrated punches and kicks do more damage and follow your body's natural dynamics. They are also harder to anticipate and you can get a lot of them in quickly.

5. Target the solar plexus, the chest area between the ribs. Here a blow with a sharp object (an umbrella, an elbow) may have a powerful immobilizing impact.

6. Another weak spot is the elbow joint. Strike it with the palm of your hand, while the attacker's arm is extended.

7. Jab a sharp object under the armpit, a little to the front. This too is a vulnerable area and attacks on it can inspire extreme pain. The same applies for the part of the body that runs down the side of the rib-cage.

Case Study: King's Cross Station, London
by Glen Warren

It is the rush hour. A cold, dark night. Pavements glisten greasily, headlights and street lamps pick out litter and tired faces. Commuters pour into the station. They walk fast, collars upturned. They just want to get home. To do so they must make their way past people, hanging round the station's exits and entrances, who do not possess anything that most people would recognize as a home.

Many of them are teenagers from the north. They arrive and London hits them. It is much bigger than they imagined, and its callousness, also, is massive. They try to find a place to live and a job. But you can't get work without an address. And you can't pay a month's rent in advance without regular work. A lot of them drift back to the railway station and its environs: its alleyways where people sleep in cardboard boxes, its sour hostels and bed and breakfast hotels. And there they get to know the long-term inhabitants of London's fringe world and from them they learn some interesting habits. They beg. They take hard drugs. They drink. Male and female, they sell their bodies in doorways for a few pounds.

Slowly but steadily they become more and more desperate. Earlier this evening one of them tried to mug a man in a side road adjoining the station entrance. The man struggled. A knife flashed, a reflex stab: it didn't have much force or go very deep, but the man still went down, hand clutching his slashed fingers. The assailant panicked and ran, blood splashes on his trousers, not a penny richer than before. Nobody tried to stop him and it was a while before anyone helped his victim. Most people were in a hurry – someone else would sort it out.

With little means of escape, a few of these youngsters will end up with the old drunks who stagger about the area. These winos sit on the kerb, lie in doorways, or reel about the pavement barging into pedestrians. They shout loudly, threatening with slurred incoherence. Nobody understands a word – not even them. Each word barges into the next, the meaning jumbled. Always aggressive, always drunk, they invariably clasp a bottle: meths with cider or wine. Methylated spirits is a potent substance. It rots the guts and the soul. The manufacturers put something in it which makes it taste foul, which makes you throw up. The veterans kill that taste with cider or wine and get an extra strong kick. At night they gather around the brightness of the station, its burger bars and kebab houses. Things have to be paid for and they hustle for money, developing an instinct for when the police are around.

A woman emerges from a burger joint. A drunk lurches in front of her, close to, arms outstretched. She can't get past. He grins, showing black, rotting teeth with gaps here and there.

'Hello, darling,' he leers, slurring in an attempt at suavity. Horror shows on her face. Charm not working, he shoves his features even closer to hers. 'Gimme money,' he snarls. She recoils. Shoving his palm under her nose, he repeats the demand. Dropping the change from her meal – a note and some silver – into his hand, she scuttles round him and hurries away. Counting the money, he shouts 'Slag' after her as a matter of course, then stumbles towards the off-licence.

All this rich, bustling life twists its way round the surrounding streets and that other feature of the locality – the women who work the streets. No matter what happens they always look bored. It is their version of machismo. And it is the younger ones, paradoxically, who look least excited about it all. Nobody can look as superbly, professionally bored as a nineteen-year-old who has sexually serviced hundreds of men. The older, most experienced girls display more wariness beneath the boredom.

The prostitutes hang about in twos and threes, their movements dictated by a close working knowledge of whether and exactly where police officers are evident. Cars cruise, men appear from side streets, transactions are made. A brunette in a zipped biker's jacket, oily hair pulled back hard, leans through the open window of a car. Her Lycra-clad legs are long and muscular above calf-length leather boots. She sweeps her hair with her hand, restlessly, as negotiations take place, her nose ring glistening. She wiggles her tightly sheathed buttocks as men pass by. Then a deal is struck, the car door opens. She slides in, a controlled smile on her lips; the car pulls away.

Around her people still flood towards the station. Work finished, they are eager to get home. All they have to do, as they head for the trains, is keep their eyes and ears very, very open.

Technology

Ingenious defensive devices are often advertised. Examples are mechanisms which spray attackers with identifying fluids. Many of these are prohibited by statute and they do not protect you from attack once an incident has actually begun, and they may be turned against you if the attacker gets a grip on them.

The best technological implements, for self-protection, are simple shriek alarms. They are widely available. They usually produce high-pitched noises of between 100 and 130 decibels. Some operate electronically and others through compressed air or gas. The compressor type are generally preferable: they tend to be less expensive. Remember, though, that compessor-type shriek alarms may need refilling. Always carry the alarm with you. When you feel insecure, perhaps on a dark street, carry the alarm in your hand – not in your handbag or pocket. It is useless to carry a screamer buried amidst your possessions, so that you cannot reach it in time.

The Suzy Lamplugh Trust sells its own screamers. Diana Lamplugh comments: 'Just carrying an alarm in your hand is a marvellous aid to confidence. It is a reminder to be alert, aware of where you are going. You also know that you can bring it up sharply by any assailant's ear – this is the only place they are likely to feel pain and it will be excruciating. Do not hesitate; the noise which you have been expecting will shock you into action. Get going and walk away as fast as you can. As you feel more mobile break into a jog if you can and seek help. Look for a garage, a pub, an open shop, a police station, somewhere there are people and a phone.'

The Law

1. Defence of the Person

You are legally entitled to use force in self-defence, providing you can show the force used was reasonable and necessary. The amount of force involved should be proportionate to the threat. To continue attacking someone, for instance, after you had knocked them out, would probably be seen as excessive force, even though they may initially have posed a grave threat to your safety.

A valid claim of self-defence can even include occasions on which you struck the first blow, although in most cases self-defence is taken to mean that the other person struck first. Normally the law requires that you show you were reluctant to fight.

Apart from the above considerations, each case is different, and different factors will be assessed when judging whether somebody acted legitimately in self-defence.

The basic law of self-defence may be complicated by recent court judgements, in murder cases involving domestic violence, where 'provocation' has been accepted as a defence for very serious assaults. These matters are currently under review and involve technicalities beyond the scope of this book.

2. Defence of Property

The same principles apply as in self-defence. Everything depends on whether 'reasonable' force is used.

3. Offensive Weapons

It is illegal, whilst in a public place, to have an offensive weapon in your possession.

An offensive weapon is anything made or adapted for the purpose of causing injury to a person, or which the possessor or some other person intends to use to cause personal injury to someone. Three different categories of weapon are identified: weapons made for causing injury, those adapted for that end, and others which an individual simply intended to use in causing such injury.

The main legislation involved is the Prevention of Crimes Act 1953. This was strengthened by the Criminal Justice Act 1988, which attempted to broaden the definition of items 'made' or 'adapted' for use as an offensive weapon. To some extent folding pocket-knives with blades shorter than 3 inches are exempt, although these obviously are covered by those parts of the legislation which stress intent and adaptation.

An acceptable defence is that the item was intended for use at work, or for religious purposes, or as part of national dress. The defendant must provide decisive evidence of this.

In practice virtually any object can be defined as an offensive weapon, under these definitions.

Personal equipment such as keys, cosmetic sprays, bags, etc. may be used in self-defence, providing excessive force is not involved and that they were carried innocently – that is to say, you did not take them with you for violent purposes. Proving such things can be very difficult, depending on the circumstances.

The general rule is simple. It is not a good idea to carry weapons. Not only can they be turned against you, but they can also get you into serious trouble. Instead use a shriek alarm, which is legally acceptable and whose function is to warn, deter, and give you added confidence; it will help to 'trigger' you into action when something happens. Do not rely on a shriek alarm to attract attention – it is by no means certain that people will respond.

PERSONAL SAFETY IN SPECIFIC AREAS

On the Street

Case Study: the Street Yob

Robert is the sort of person who is likely to give you trouble on the street. Indeed, his whole eighteen-year-old body seems to be organized, to the point of parody, around the Trouble Principle. No hair, as if it has been machine-gunned back into his skull, is discernible on the surface of his head. Beneath is a heavy face, limbs that move jerkily. And the clothes, with their fashionable circus-clown bagginess, suggest violence in a different way: as if they are a rejection of the whole possibility of order and symmetry and the restraint that they imply.

Robert himself is unequivocal on the matter: 'I dress how I like, talk how I like, go where I like. If people don't fancy it that's their problem.' He has no doubts either about how street violence begins. 'Respect. That's what the game is all about. People have to show you respect.' And what is respect? 'Respect is getting out of your way when you come by. It means not giving you dirty looks, not shoving you out of the way in the pub, not cutting you up on a corner when you're driving, not jumping ahead of you in a queue, not trying it on with your bird, not taking the piss in general.'

Those foolish enough to be disrespectful are not given a second chance: 'I had five brothers and sisters, sharing two bedrooms. That taught you about looking after yourself, keeping your end up. Outside the front door, where we lived, it was even worse. It was the sort of place where you had to have front. If you didn't, kids just took the piss. They'd treat you like shit. It was a good lesson and it's still the same. If anybody tries it on they get a clouting from me and that's it. It's the only way. Show weakness and people shit all over you.' The message which Robert and his friends derive from their lives is clear: violence is the fast-track route for those who want a tolerable life in the techno-mess of the inner city.

And the normal restraints just do not count: 'There's nothing much to lose. The courts are a joke. You can half kill someone and walk off with a fine and probation. And even if the judge gets heavy and I have to do a bit of bird, so what? What am I missing when I'm behind bars? I'm never going to have a proper job. All the factory jobs that kept my dad and his mates in work for years have gone and they're not coming back. The people who run the country don't give a shit about people like me.' Although he pretends to be detached there is a degree of self-pity in his character. And this comes out as resentment: 'I've got to admit I really get pissed off when I see these smart-arse types with their briefcases and suits. People like that. They've had everything given to them. Not all of them. Some of them have worked for it. But most of them are just people who've had everything done for them. And then they come round areas like this. Not because they want to live here, with riff-raff like us, but because the houses are cheap. It really gets me when I see those types.'

As he speaks the muscular body flexes itself, as if to hint at the force with which the resentments, and the obvious touchiness, can be backed up. And everything about him reinforces a point so obvious that, like most obvious points, it can be easily and disastrously forgotten: he is too young, and too stubborn, to be impressed by anything as flimsy, as easily kicked aside, as reason. This means it is very difficult to get through to him in the ordinary way. His inaccessibility, to all outside his immediate age-group and locality, makes him both unpredictable and frightening. Robert is not someone you would want to be close to for very long on a street corner.

Men of all ages, contrary to popular belief, are more at risk from street attack than women, as has already been noted. They face a double threat, both from those who rob for gain and from those who indulge in violence and harassment for their own sake. Males are more likely to be seen as legitimate targets: for a street thug there is no particular status to be gained from attacking a woman. Yet attacking a man, however unequal the actual contest, is much more likely to be viewed as evidence of toughness. Even during a mugging attackers will use greater force against men, as males are considered more likely to offer physical resistance. So adult men, as well as others, should note the advice given below. This is aimed particularly at those who are on their own: those in groups are much less at risk. Risks of all kinds are of course greater on the street when it is dark.

We obviously emphasize action to take when things go wrong. This does not mean that things often go wrong. Most people will be safe most of the time, although it is still worth being aware of the risks and of ways of neutralizing them.

1. Note the information given earlier on the importance of preparation. When you are on the street know where you are going and why. Observe what is going on around you. This does not mean that your whole life is controlled by a schedule. Nor does it mean that you exude the sort of wariness that actually creates hostility in those around you. What you should develop is a state of relaxed alertness, of easygoing purposefulness, so that you are ready, but not over-ready, for any problems that may occur.

2. Think about the sort of street you are on and its neighbourhood. Develop a 'mind map' so that you are conscious of the often subtle but vital differences between particular roads or environments. Different localities will present different problems. Is the street you are on near large public housing estates? Are there obvious signs of decay and neglect: stray dogs, litter, abandoned cars? How far are you from a main road, from a telephone box, from a cab office, from a police station?

3. Avoid dark streets and alleyways, stretches of deserted open ground, long or badly lit subways.

4. Do not take short cuts if they involve going through lonely places late at night.

5. At night stick to the routes you know. If someone suggests a short cut check it out first during the day.

6. If you are on a dark street at night, walk in the centre of the pavement, away from walls, hidden doorways and bushes.

7. If possible, walk on the side of the road that faces oncoming traffic. Look confident. Walk at a good pace, as if you know where you are going. But do not hurry. Hurry, to some street people, suggests either the tension of a potential victim or the arrogance of a transgressor who is intruding on what they regard as *their* territory.

8. Clothing and footwear are important. If you are planning to enter difficult areas do not wear garments that restrict your movement or that attract undue attention. Good solid shoes, which help your balance and in which you can move quickly, are to be recommended.

9. Do not be seen consulting maps or guidebooks, or openly asking directions. Any suggestion that you do not know your way around indicates you might be a target. Guidebooks can be looked at in doorways or in shops, away from the general gaze. Ask shopkeepers or office staff for directions, rather than people in the street: you will often get better advice and will attract less attention.

10. Be aware of strangers who are near you, without appearing nervous or aggressive, and without attracting their attention. In volatile, inner city areas and many other places, the more troublesome individuals can be very touchy about people scrutinizing them. If you are worried do not stare. Do not stop and turn your head at intervals. Instead use reflections in shop windows: they will reveal whether someone is following or watching you. Another method is to halt and fiddle with a shoelace or an item of clothing. It is natural for people to look round at such times. Crossing a road also provides an excellent excuse to study your surroundings with care, without being conspicuous as you do so.

11. If you feel you are being followed, especially late at night, the first thing is to establish whether your suspicions are correct. Where possible use the techniques described immediately above. Cross and recross the road to see if the person stays with you.

If they persist head towards the nearest bright lights or occupied building.

12. If a car is following you, turn and walk or run fast back in its direction. The driver will find it hard to turn the car to pursue you.

13. Do not accept lifts from people you do not know. If, when you are in an unfamiliar locality, a stranger stops in a car, and asks if you need help with directions, tell them decisively but politely that you know where you are going.

14. Street assaults or muggings do not always begin in a clear-cut manner. Quite often a tentative initial approach is made. You are asked for the time or for directions, or somebody 'requests' money in a vaguely menacing way, or perhaps your appearance and dress are the subject of loud comment.

It is at these points that you are assessed as a target. This early sparring also gives the less confident assailant time to develop some courage or a sense of indignation. It additionally allows him maximum opportunity to extricate himself if he loses his nerve. If someone intervenes, the aggressor can pretend he was just teasing or indulging in horseplay.

If you appear weak or indecisive a move may be made. Your bag will be snatched, you will be invited to surrender money at knife-point, blows will be delivered . . .

All depends on the messages radiated by your behaviour. An appearance of decisiveness and firmness increases your chances at this stage. Keep walking. Look confident, as if you know where you are going. Be polite. Do not be provocative, but do not, also, look as if you can easily be pushed around.

15. You should know your own priorities. If trouble starts you should either make an effective defence of yourself or else you should run as far and fast as you can. The worst thing is indecisiveness.

Many safety authorities advise that self-preservation is the main priority, so that you immediately surrender any valuables. Obviously you have the right to self-defence and to resist attempts to rob you. It is up to you to decide what option you take in a given set of circumstances. Most people would agree that it is more important to protect yourself than to hang on to material goods at all costs.

16. A shriek alarm (a 'screamer') is useful in virtually all eventualities, whether you choose to run or fight. See the comments about this in the section on Technology, above.

17. Be careful about how much you drink. Alcohol affects your judgement. It makes you over-confident and simultaneously also slows your reactions.

18. Often bag-snatchers will make themselves known to you with great speed. The snatcher runs toward or past you, clutching the strap of the bag as he draws level. However, pickpockets frequently operate in a more complicated style and you will encounter them in a small team. One of the team will bump you or jostle you. When, in response, you check your clothing or bags this reveals where you keep valuables. Then one of them bumps you, distracting your attention while an accomplice grabs your purse, wallet or bag.
    There are several overlapping techniques which help you to cope with the threat from snatchers and pocket-pickers:

a. As noted earlier, if you carry your bag with the straps across your chest you may be dragged along, and may simply inspire an attacker to use greater force. A good idea is to carry a 'decoy' bag containing a few less valuable items, which you can surrender if you have no choice; important items can be kept elsewhere on your person, or under your coat in a bag. Keep all bag compartments buttoned or zipped. Visible bags should be held in front of you or tightly beneath the arm; this applies to strapped briefcases and camera bags as much as it does to shoulder bags.
b. When possible use a money belt, worn next to the skin, for really important items.
c. If you carry considerable amounts of cash divide it up, so that it is spread through several pockets.

d. Your cheque card and cheque book should be separate from each other, so that a thief cannot use the cheque book.

e. Security briefcases are available; these have alarms which activate when grabbed by a thief.

f. Do not carry house and car keys in your bag; put them in a pocket, preferably not an outside pocket.

g. Do not put keys next to items carrying your name and address.

h. During the day, in high-risk areas, walk near to the wall (not too close to the wall – walk too close and you will look as if you have something to hide), so that any bags or other items which you carry are accessible only from one side; do not do this on isolated streets at night – at such times it is safest to walk in the middle of the pavement, where you are visible and away from doorways and hidden entrances.

At Home

Domestic violence is an extremely important topic and it is vital that individuals learn to cope with the threat and actuality of its occurrence. The word 'occurrence' is, however, a problem here. For it is one of those highly politicized crime issues that can easily be exaggerated beyond all recognition. This creates a lot of unnecessary fear and social tension. The two main techniques, used in this distortion, are the Portmanteau method and the Leading Question stratagem. The first of these involves stretching the definition of domestic violence so far that virtually any behaviour, from breakfast table rudeness to mild teasing, can be included in the figures along with the most appalling assaults. The Leading Question stratagem is usually deployed in the course of formal research projects into the phenomenon. A small number of people are asked if they have experienced domestic violence. The problem, apart from the tiny sample, the wide definition used, and the self-selecting nature of the respondents ('victims' are more likely to participate), is that the questions are framed so as to elicit certain answers and to avoid others. Another major difficulty is that respondents' allegations are largely taken at face value.

Much of this research is, then, no more than glorified opinion-polling in which the subjective responses of a handful of people are accorded enormous significance. We have all seen the results: headlines declaring that some huge percentage of the populace has suffered domestic assault. It is only at the bottom of the page that we read the even more terrible facts: the in-depth academic research was based solely on the untested opinions of 83 people interviewed in Hartlepool.

Some people might say that this does not matter. Surely domestic violence is so nasty that anything which draws attention to it is permissible. Yet the pump-priming exaggeration actually damages attempts to deal with the real problem. For the distortion finally becomes so obvious that people stop listening; they refuse even to pay attention to the real cases, which are serious enough. And exaggeration also hinders attempts to arrive at constructive answers to the subject as it actually exists.

The point deserves repetition. Domestic assaulters do not lurk behind every set of curtains. The nation's living-rooms do not reverberate every evening to the sound of violent assault. There is, however, a real problem and it is best approached from a rational rather than an over heated viewpoint.

Those directly exposed to domestic violence, or who are aware of it happening in their vicinity, should note the following.

1. Domestic violence is now taken far more seriously than before. Complaints have a much better chance of getting a response, from both official agencies and individuals.

2. There is considerable evidence to suggest that men, often at the hands of women, also suffer in this way. It is quite likely that social pressures and stereotyping make it difficult for males to report cases. Additionally, they are less likely than women to be received sympathetically when they do complain. Nonetheless there is growing awareness that the problem of domestic violence crosses gender boundaries; and men who are subjected to real abuse should try to get some sort of help from the appropriate organizations.

3. Over the last few years police organizations have come under pressure to do something about general domestic abuse. They have made a considerable response, at least in terms of money and resources. Many forces have set up special units and training programmes. Far more facilities, as a result, are available for the assistance of victims.

4. There are numerous non-police organizations, such as Victim Support, which take a close interest in the question of domestic assault. Local authorities, women's refuges and support networks are included amongst them. A number of these are listed in the Reference Section of this book (p. 259).

5. Those who are immediately under threat should use the sections of this book which deal with techniques for avoiding and coping with aggression.

Case Study: Domestic Violence

Jill, aged forty-seven, has been married to Steve, who is a few years older, for twelve years. They have two pre-pubescent children. She is a teacher and her husband is in marketing. They are now in the process of divorcing (the names of the participants have been changed).

She says: 'Things started to get bad when Steve was promoted. His new job was actually easier than the old one. He had to travel less and could delegate things to his subordinates. He had a bigger office and lots more money. But it didn't seem to make him any happier. He'd always been moody. Now he became bloody impossible. At first it was just verbal bullying. He'd come home from work and pick a row over just about anything. Anything at all. The kids were really small then and they were terrified of his shouting. But the real horror began one weekend when the kids were at my mother's. A Saturday afternoon after we came back from the supermarket. He just started on me without warning. Afterwards I was covered in bruises. All over my lower torso. That was the amazing thing. He'd look like he'd totally lost control but later you'd realize he'd calculated it so that no marks showed on the face or the legs. It was awful.

And afterwards I could hardly even remember what bloody started it. That was the most amazing bit. Usually the flashpoint was something incredibly trivial. It was terrible. I felt so degraded. It just kept happening and I couldn't think of what to do. In a second he would change from this perfectly nice man into some sort of lunatic. Afterwards he would just sit there calmly and deny it, or say that I exaggerated it. And he was so cunning. He seemed to choose moments when there were fewest potential witnesses. When the kids were at my mother's or round their friends'. Then the next day he'd troop off to work as if nothing had happened.

'Things came to a head when I said I was going. That I simply couldn't take any more. That shook him. For a few years it settled down. Sometimes I got a clout and he still lost his temper verbally, but it was under control. I wasn't happy. But I suppose I still loved him. Then when my little boy went to prep school it all started again. This time he used to use a wet towel. Like something out of a crime novel when the attacker doesn't want to leave marks. I remember thinking he must have read it in one of the thrillers he liked. Using a wet towel. It doesn't leave marks. It was crazy. I remember thinking about that when he was beating me once. You get these surreal, detached thoughts, even when someone is beating shit out of you. I put up with a month of weekend beatings. These sharp repeated blows, mostly to the thighs and back, with the towel or the flat of the hand. And it was always so controlled. That was what I couldn't work out. How he'd virtually be frothing at the mouth and yet the blows were so controlled. And then he would be so contrite. He no longer tried to pretend it didn't happen. There were all the corny excuses about work pressure, about things getting better if we just gave it time, etc. And then I left. I took my little girl, collected the boy from school and went to my mother's. I haven't seen him since. He's never tried to come after me. We talk through solicitors and he's agreed to the basic divorce terms. He knows if he was awkward I'd bring up all the stuff about the beatings. The funny thing was, my mother had no idea. Not a clue about the real reason. I couldn't bring myself to tell her. I felt degraded, ashamed. I can't believe my own feelings. He'd done all that to me and I felt ashamed.'

Shopping Centres

Modern shopping is increasingly conducted in large shopping centres, rather than in the traditional high street. These environments have a great many attractions for the potential thief and the street yob. They contain a high concentration of very desirable consumer goods in an exciting and comfortable setting. They cost nothing to enter, are open most of the day, and it is difficult to restrict access. It is inevitable therefore that many such places attract gangs of youths, eager to impress bypassers with their bravado.

1. If you use a shopping centre regularly think about where, within it, the rowdy element most often gathers. This does not mean that you avoid such places, simply that you take reasonable precautions in certain locations (see the entries above about awareness and self-protection).

2. Work out where the security staff and senior management are located within the complex.

3. If security is poor, or there are severe problems with rowdiness, raise the question with local crime prevention groups and with shopping centre management. If necessary go straight to the police.

4. The best time to bring up security issues is at the planning stage. If local authorities are planning a shopping centre development, get involved in the process of public consultation. Simultaneously raise the matter through police-community consultative groups.

Town Centres

Town centres, especially the newer ones, raise similar problems to those encountered in shopping centres. At times their very environmental attractiveness is counter-productive. It can simply draw people who want a nice arena in which to display their yobbishness. As with shopping centres the shrewd citizen, through the right kind of participation at the right time, can influence events.

1. Ensure that crime and personal safety are included in planning processes whenever there is consultation over new town centre developments; the same applies when refurbishment or upgrading are planned for established sites. Here the merits of closed-circuit television (CCTV), as a surveillance device and a deterrent, are worthy of consideration. Obviously its usage raises serious and controversial questions concerning the rights of citizens. Some commentators are very much against its widespread use. Others take the opposite view. Diana Lamplugh of the Suzy Lamplugh Trust, however, has few doubts about the matter: 'CCTV has proved to be very effective indeed, not only for monitoring criminal intent, but also for identifying potential and actual perpetrators. The very presence of these closed-circuit television cameras ensured a significant reduction of reported crimes wherever they have been installed. When the introduction of CCTV is challenged by the civil rights lobby we would be wise to consider whose rights need protecting most.'

2. Develop an awareness of which parts of the location, at which times, are most volatile.

3. At night plan your movements when you go through the town centre.

4. Ensure you know how near you are to telephone boxes and to escape routes.

Case Study: Town Centres

A description of a town centre, in south-east England, by a former resident:

'I moved there to work and it was an old market town, with this shopping centre and car-parks dumped at one end. Round the outside was a ring road and at night, when you crossed the ring road, and went into the centre, it was like being on the moon. There was nobody. Not a soul. But then things changed. The council approved some fast food joints and a video store. Let them open up, till late in the evening, on the fringe of the shopping centre which also expanded a bit. And they added these extra pedestrianized sections. Before you knew it half the kids from outlying villages and suburbs were in there every night. You used to find condoms and plastic bags with glue on them. My mate even swore he saw a girl of about thirteen having it off in a doorway. In a doorway! Early one evening. With yobs standing about and watching. You heard lots of stories like that.

'I knew there was a lot going on but I didn't really listen. That was a mistake. One weekend my brother came down and we went for a walk through the centre. It was a Sunday and it was as quiet as a morgue. That was until we turned this corner and there, pissed out of their minds, was this gang of about a dozen yobs. Any age from fifteen to twenty. And the bastards chased us. All round the fucking car-park, round the pedestrian precinct and across the ring road. It must have looked ridiculous. Real Keystone Cops stuff. But we were scared shitless and they would have knocked hell out of us. They only stopped when one of them called out something about how he thought he'd seen a cop car or something. But that was it for me. I never went through that damn place after dark again. Even on my way back from the pub. And the first chance I got I took a transfer out of there.'

Public Transport

When you are using public transport the points made earlier, about planning and preparation, and about the differences in neighbouring localities, are especially appropriate. A bus or train may pass through a variety of areas on a short journey; each locality will contain different types of people who may become your fellow passengers.

People will get on your bus or train bringing their area, and its mannerisms, with them, as it were, and they will be harder to escape than normally. You may find yourself in shoulder-bumping contact with individuals you would not normally want to be anywhere near.

Staff shortages and funding policies mean, also, that there are fewer conductors, guards and other transport workers to help you. Your own reactions and preparations therefore will be extremely important. To reduce the risks follow the advice given below:

1. Study bus and train routes and connections; aim to avoid waiting too long in lonely or late-night locations; learn about alternative routes in case something goes wrong.

2. When driving to a station or pick-up point think about where you will park; leave the car in a properly lit place, as near to the train or bus as possible.

3. Always bring coins and a telephone card in case there are problems.

4. While waiting for connections keep to well-lit areas; work out where the escape routes and telephone boxes are, and the nearest places you can find help in an emergency.

5. On a train ensure you know the location of the emergency handle.

6. Check how many escape routes, from the bus or train carriage, there are that you can easily reach.

7. If possible sit near doors and aisles.

8. Where possible sit in a busy carriage. On a bus, especially at night, sit downstairs; if you must sit upstairs do not sit at the back: upstairs at the back is where the trouble-makers often congregate.

9. Ensure valuables are not visible and keep bags and cases near you.

10. Be careful if somebody offers to help with luggage.

11. Request proof of identity if you are suspicious of a person who claims to be a member of the transport system staff.

12. Study your surroundings when waiting at a main-line bus or train station. You will soon notice the variety of individuals who are obviously just hanging around; many of them are harmless, but others are in pursuit of various unsavoury goals. Most of them will confine themselves, most of the time, to certain informal but clearly defined territories within the station: some for instance will patrol an area in and around the gents' lavatory, others will congregate near off-licences, or will beg outside cafés. Discreet observation will soon teach you which parts of the terminal to avoid or to treat with caution.

13. Young people are especially at risk from some of the figures who drift about a busy transport terminal; many of these places are notorious for attempts to pick up young runaways or truants who are then inducted into prostitution or deviant sub-cultures. It is up to parents to warn children about the dangers, and the police should be immediately alerted if children are seen in the company of suspicious individuals at such places.

Minicabs and Taxis

Legal controls on cabs and taxis depend on location. Outside London 'private hire cars' are licensed and drivers are vetted. They are not allowed to cruise in search of business and can only be booked on the telephone or via their office. Black taxis in London are licensed by the police. Licence numbers are displayed on the inside and outside of the cab. The driver must wear a badge which can easily be seen.

However, there are no licensing controls over minicabs operating in London. Most of the drivers involved are competent and trustworthy. Yet growing concern has been expressed about the risks created by the behaviour of a small number of such drivers. The following advice should be noted.

1. Use a reputable company, especially one recommended by friends or those who know about such things.

2. Make your booking by telephone; ensure you know the driver's name, call sign, and make of car.

3. Do not take rides with cabs which tout for custom in the street; some drivers are freelance but pretend to work for companies and simply hang around transport terminals with fake aerials and radio equipment. Always book by telephone.

4. When calling from a public place keep your voice low, so that you are not overheard, and so that nobody tries to trick you by impersonating the cab driver; when the cab driver arrives check his details, as in point number 2. above.

5. It is safer and cheaper to share a cab with a friend, especially if you both get out at the same point.

6. Chatting to the driver gives you the chance to assess him and to detect anything unsettling about him; however, do not reveal personal details.

7. Always sit in the rear of the car, near the door, on the side opposite the driver's side.

8. If at any point you are worried about the driver's behaviour ask him to stop the car, preferably at a spot which is populous and/or well-lit; get out, pay the appropriate fare and leave as fast as you can.

9. Never linger when you reach your destination; pay the fare quickly in cash, and have your keys ready so that you can get into your home without delay.

In Your Car

The car as a suit of armour: increasingly, many people have opted out of street life and both its real and imagined risks. It is ironic that their preferred alternative, car travel, should recently have become a focus of concern regarding crime and personal safety. As often, the dangers are exaggerated, and traffic accidents are a far greater hazard for motorists than assault. Some motoring organizations have rightly been criticized for exaggerating such fears, in attempts to sell cellular car phones and other devices.

Many men, also, feel resentful that bodies like the AA give queue-jumping priority, at no extra charge, to lone women who have broken down, even in built-up areas during the day. 'I think it's a cheek,' said one man. 'Why should I pay the same membership rates as a woman for a second-rate service, just because of the remote chance that she might be in danger, especially when statistically men are more likely to be at risk?' This sort of discrimination is also wide open to trickery, with women sending their passengers off to the nearest pub or café so that they can pretend to be alone when the AA man arrives.

These questions aside, there are certain clear-cut precautions which should be acted on when driving.

1. Regular maintenance makes it less likely that your car will break down in some hostile environment.

2. It is a good idea to carry extra petrol in a portable can, plus an emergency puncture aerosol.

3. If stationary in traffic, or parked for a while, keep the windows locked, or as high as possible; keep the doors locked.

4. Valuables and bags should be out of sight.

5. Carry comprehensive and up-to-date guidebooks and maps so that you do not need to stop for directions.

Motorways

There is no common school of thought about what to do if your car breaks down, or if for some other reason you are forced to stop, in the special and hazardous environment of a motorway.

Here the normal crime prevention considerations become extra complicated. Should you remain in the car, after putting a 'help' sign in the back window? Or should you walk to a telephone? If you do make a call do you return to the car? A number of fatal motorway accidents occur when a car collides with a stationary vehicle parked on the hard shoulder.)

Note the following advice:

a. If possible, drive to an emergency telephone, so that the front passenger door is level with the telephone as much to the left as is practicable.

b. Put on the hazard lights.

c. Only use the nearside door when leaving the car.

d. Do not reverse the car to a telephone.

e. Do not cross any part of the motorway to get to a more convenient telephone.

f. Telephones on motorways are located at one mile intervals, with marker posts every 100 metres indicating the distances.

g. Money is not needed to work the telephones. They ring in the police control room as soon as the handset is raised; they also automatically tell the police your location.

h. When using the phone you should look towards the oncoming cars.

i. Give all relevant details to the control room, including the car's distance from the telephone.

j. Many experts advise that you should stay at the telephone and not return to the car unless you have no other option (i.e. if you are in immediate danger or if exposure to extreme cold outweighs other risks).

k. Check, when the breakdown truck appears, that the driver knows your details and has been sent officially; 'pirate' breakdown vehicles cruise for custom on many motorways.

l. Do not lock the passenger door if you leave the car, so that you can get in again in a hurry; but lock all other doors and the windows.

m. If you wait in the car ensure all doors and windows are secure.

n. When you are on the telephone give police the registration number of any cars that pull up near you.

o. Never leave keys in the car.

p. Stay out of sight if you are waiting on the bank of the motorway.

Cycling

Cyclists are more vulnerable than motorists, for obvious reasons, although sometimes they seem to forget this. Take the advice below when riding through risky areas:

1. Ride fast but not recklessly.

2. Do not ride on the pavement: this is dangerous in ordinary circumstances, but is even more so when there are lots of touchy individuals about.

3. Look alert and efficient – it helps if your bike is clean and well maintained.

4. It is useful to have a loud horn or a whistle or screamer.

5. Ensure you can lock the bike properly if you must leave it.

6. Carry spare cash so that you can get home if the bike malfunctions.

Safety at Work

Personal safety and crime prevention at work are topics which have recently been given considerable attention. Such problems cost employers a great deal of time and money. They also physically and mentally traumatize employees and dramatically reduce their efficiency. Authorities like the Suzy Lamplugh Trust, the London School of Economics and the Health and Safety Executive have produced interesting material on these issues. Below are summarized some of the main precautions which employees should take.

Job Search

You are particularly vulnerable when seeking work. Your natural protective responses, by definition, will be relatively muted. Getting a job means being open, flexible and anxious to please. Unscrupulous individuals and groups can easily capitalize on these attributes and can distort them for their own purposes.

1. Try to check out the credentials of advertised jobs, especially where the details provided about those offering the jobs are incomplete.

2. This applies also to recruiting agencies; assess their reputation, and whether they properly vet work premises and client organizations.

3. Be suspicious of extravagant claims and financial promises. Remember: if it looks too good to be true the chances are it is too good to be true . . .

4. Any interviews should be conducted on the premises of the firm directly concerned or their immediate representatives or agents.

5. If this is not possible insist on meeting in a public place.

6. If you are worried arrange for a friend to wait nearby.

7. Do not attend any interview about which you are really uneasy.

8. Let a friend know the interview time and when you plan to get home.

9. If it is late in the evening or early in the morning arrange for someone to collect you; if friends or relatives are unavailable get a cab to pick you up and ensure that someone you know is able to check that you have returned.

10. In the interview avoid the sort of personal topics and questions that are not directly connected with the main subject.

11. Think carefully before continuing the interview socially, in a pub or restaurant; have appropriate excuses ready. Do not go to someone's home, and if you do go to a bar or restaurant ensure you telephone people to let them know about your changed arrangements.

12. Do not let the interviewer drive you anywhere.

13. Insist that the job terms and specifications are made absolutely clear; be wary of any vagueness about these matters.

14. You should make even greater efforts to cover the above points if you are considering work overseas; the prospect of foreign employment, by definition, will be harder to assess, especially regarding travel and accommodation.

At the Work Site

A surprising number of assaults and thefts actually occur at the work-place itself. Perhaps those most at risk are people who come into frequent contact with the general public. Yet such problems occur in all different vocational arenas. The answer, as always, is found in a little common-sense planning and preparation. The aim is not to fill people with trepidation, but to indicate the sort of general approach that will make work easier and more relaxed. If you are prepared, you will cope better on the few occasions when something does go severely wrong. You will also cope better with the fear of such problems, which is far more pervasive than the problems themselves.

1. Money should not be left lying around on desks or machinery; nor should it be left in or with discarded clothing. The same applies to valuables such as cameras and personal tape recorders.

2. When possible store briefcases and bags in locked cupboards and cabinets.

3. Home telephone numbers and addresses should only be given to trusted and established clients. Unless the circumstances are exceptional do not provide such details for people you do not know well. Those who are ex-directory face fewer problems, as giving their number does not mean that they are also giving a means of working out their address, through the telephone book.

Visitors

1. Decide whom you would report to if somebody suspicious entered your work-place.

2. If a stranger who worries you does appear, ask them if you can help them, without being unnecessarily obtrusive.

3. Report them to the appropriate person if you think they are in any way likely to be trouble. Establish whether there is a set routine, within the organization, for dealing with such eventualities.

4. Find out if there is a system, in your work-place, for checking the credentials of service and trades staff who visit (delivery people, computer engineers, heating engineers, window cleaners, etc.). If no such system exists persuade your bosses to initiate one.

5. Do not surrender equipment for maintenance to people who say they are service and repair staff unless you have first established that this has been approved by your superiors.

6. Do not let unfamiliar visitors get hold of your contact details (especially your home address) and work schedules; make sure they do not overhear you giving such information to others.

Assault

Physical threat and actual assault at work can cause severe problems for those unprepared for them.

1. Do not assume, if you are attacked, that workmates and others will automatically come to your assistance. They may do so, but you cannot rely on it: most people are traumatized by sudden outbreaks of violence or hostility, wherever they occur, and are simply not ready to respond in a constructive manner.

2. Do take the trouble, in the light of this, to discuss the issue with your colleagues, especially if you are in an occupation which brings you into contact with people who are unruly. See if you can reach agreement with your workmates about how to co-operate if trouble occurs. Do not be over-ambitious. Settle for a simple understanding that somebody phones the police, that somebody else acts simultaneously as witness of the incident, that somebody routinely checks the first aid equipment, and that simple escape routes are always available. This sort of informal planning boosts morale and also makes it more likely that people will be genuinely helpful in a crisis.

3. Think about your working environment. What are the chief characteristics of its particular workers and clients? Identify the specific types of individuals who are most likely to help you and also those who might be a threat. Think about the layout of the building or buildings: are there any heavy objects that might be used aggressively, for instance; where are the nearest portering or security staff; is there a telephone within reach; what is the quickest way out of the building?

4. If someone looks as though they are about to attack, ensure that you are not alone with them. Go as fast as possible to where there are eye-witnesses and where you can get help.

5. If, however, you persuade the person or persons to calm down a little it might, on occasion, be helpful if you got them away from the audience, as mentioned earlier, (fear of losing face before an audience may be a big influence on aggressive behaviour) with the aim of talking them completely out of their aggression. Do not do this unless you are sure of what you are about, and ensure that you remain within reach of others.

6. Any violent incidents or threats, however small, should be reported to management or to union representatives. The larger the firm, the more important it is that this is done. Big firms are complex. You cannot leave it to chance that management are fully aware of everything that happens in the work-place. Bringing things to their attention may mean that such issues are considered at a high level. Hopefully they will then become part of the organization's 'safety agenda'.

Going Out

Problems can also arise, during work-time, when employees are away from the the office or factory.

1. Leave a record of your destination, expected time of arrival there, and the likely time of your return.

2. Do not make appointments with strangers unless you have good reason to believe that they are reputable. Always meet them in a public place and do not go somewhere private with them.

3. If your plans change, while you are out, ensure that your office knows.

4. If you are unhappy about someone do not get into a lift with them. If you are already in a lift and become worried, stand by the door, in reach of the alarm button, and make sure you know how the control buttons operate.

Overview

Safety and crime prevention overlap into many different areas, especially in a work environment. The design of buildings and furniture, shift systems, first aid training, assertiveness training, recruitment and retention of staff: these are just some of the issues affected by crime in the work-place. It is important, therefore, that management and staff co-operate, so that a systematic approach is taken to these problems.

The sort of questions employers and employees should examine together include:

1. Are car-parks secure and properly supervised?

2. Are isolated workers given contact numbers and advice so that they can rapidly summon help?

3. Do work spaces allow maximum visibility?

4. How easy are they for strangers to enter?

5. Do they provide a variety of exit points?

6. Are workers within easy access of telephones?

7. Are desks, for interviewing members of the public, properly positioned, and should they be fitted with panic buttons?

8. Is the lighting adequate?

9. Does the décor promote a soothing and positive atmosphere, or is it harsh and discordant?

10. Has the company arranged formal training in crime prevention and safety, and does this involve extensive contact with professionals in the field?

11. Is there a company after-care scheme for employees who have been subjected to attack, and has this been devised with the help of professional therapists?

PERSONAL SAFETY FOR SPECIFIC GROUPS

The Elderly

There is growing awareness, in our society, that age is often a very misleading guide to personal characteristics and behaviour. Many old age pensioners are physically and mentally sharper than people much younger than them.

However, a number of older individuals, particularly those living alone, are especially vulnerable. Physically they may be weaker than others; psychologically they may be isolated and out of contact with developments in their vicinity. They will be more susceptible to all types of criminal threat. In particular they are easy targets for aggressive or duplicitous door-callers.

Those in contact with such people, especially their relatives and close friends, should do all they can to ensure they are as safe as possible. Follow the guidelines below.

1. For advice on avoiding artifice burglary consult the appropriate part of this book, in the section on combating burglary.

2. Ensure that isolated older people are kept informed of events in their area, particularly concerning crime and safety. Let them know about the services, benefits and facilities open to older people.

3. Get patrolling police officers to visit them regularly.

4. See what help can be offered by local branches of Help the Aged or Age Concern.

5. Ask reliable neighbours to watch out for them and for any suspicious events in or near their home.

6. If there is a Neighbourhood Watch or tenants' association in their street, ask the watch co-ordinator or tenants' leader if they can help.

7. Of particular importance are schemes run by voluntary groups, often in conjunction with the police, to provide home security devices free or at a low cost.

8. Older people should have screamer alarms, kept within reach, both inside and outside the house. Alarms linked to telephone lines, alerting emergency services, are also available. A number of local authorities provide them free or for a small charge.

9. An attempt should be made to ensure that such householders are never alone when meter readers and other officials call. All credentials offered by these figures should be rigorously checked. If possible they should call at precise, pre-arranged times.

10. People who are at home alone should always answer the door bell. Not to do so may suggest to a criminal that nobody is at home and that it is OK to break in. A door chain should always be used. Nobody who is remotely suspicious should be allowed in.

11. A big danger is posed by those who will use every stratagem, including that of disguising themselves as officials, to gain access to a dwelling. Once inside, one of them will distract the attention of the elderly person, while the other rifles the place in search of money and valuables. All efforts must be made to warn potential victims about their activities, especially when police are aware of particular suspects who are currently operating in the area.

12. 'Knockers' are a particular menace. These are people who appear at the front door, offering to take away unwanted items, often stacked up in cellars and attics. They offer very low prices for what are sometimes valuable pieces. They will go to considerable efforts to convince the owner that the antique or painting is not worth very much and will then pay a pittance for it, despite the fact that it is actually worth much more.
    Some knockers are effectively on 'reconnaissance missions' for burglars, or they are burglars themselves 'clocking' the household for its 'stealability'.

Case Study: 'Knocking'

Dave is a knocker. Here he describes how he operates.

'I'm in the information game, really. That's the first thing. Getting that bit of knowledge. Often you just overhear a conversation, or one of your mates does. The best places are pubs, cafés, especially places frequented by blokes who have to go into houses to read meters or do repairs and all that. I've got a mate who years ago used to con his way into the works canteen at the local gas repair headquarters. Just so he could get talking to the meter readers. In the end I think he went native, started imagining he was a bloody gasman or something. All he could talk about was meters. People started calling him Gassy. Crazy the lengths people will go to for a scam. Not that he didn't know his business. I reckon at one time half the thefts in the area were down to him and his mates. All because of meter readers and their big mouths. And when you've got that bit of information then you go in. There are so many ways. One time I overheard a bloke in my local going on about some old bloke who lived in this run-down bungalow loaded with antique furniture and stuff. A few days later me and a mate parked fifty yards from his front door. We opened the bonnet so we could pretend we were trying to fix the engine. Gave us an excuse to be there, to have a look at the place. It looked all right. Scruffy, run-down, but with lots of gear visible through the windows when we drove past later on.

'A day later I came back, did the routine with the bloke. Funny thing was, he stank. Can't have washed for ages. Yet he obviously had money, judging by the gear in there. I said to him did he have any stuff to sell, anything I could take off his hands. All that. He was a classic case, swallowed it all. Inside I bought some junk off him and clocked the place while he went off to fetch some more stuff. From what I could see there were quite a few nice pieces. Even better there were no proper locks. Nothing was property marked. I had another quick look round when I went to the toilet. On the way out I asked when he might be in if I happened to call again when in the area. "All the time," he said. "Except Monday morning when I go over to my sister's place." I couldn't help smiling when he said that. As I said, he was a classic case. An hour later I was on the line to my old mate. Gave him all the vital statistics. Entrances and exits, the kind of locks he had on the front door and so on. Everything he needed to know. Including the fact that he was out all Monday morning. Within a week he was inside there. Cleaned the joint of anything nickable. And there was some tasty stuff. Candlesticks, silver cutlery, bit of jewellery, a silver snuff box, £700 in a box in the kitchen. I got a tidy little slice out of the proceeds. "Nice one", as we say round here when we want to be a bit corny . . .'

Ethnic Minorities

Over the last thirty years large ethnic minority communities have developed in the UK. Members of these groups face crime problems which differ from those of the majority population. Cultural factors, for instance, may complicate attitudes and responses to basic questions of law and order. But by far the biggest issues, in this context, are those of racial prejudice and attack themselves.

There is considerable evidence that racial abuse and racially motivated assault are serious problems. Exactly how prevalent they are is hard to judge. Some such crimes, for example when extremist groups fire-bomb ethnic community centres, or when hysterically abusive leaflets are distributed, are obvious. Yet a great many other incidents present us with the same questions of subjectivity and definition that confound attempts to quantify sexual offences in any detail. One of the hardest things is deciding someone's motivation, when there is no material evidence to indicate it either way. Motive is internal, and difficult to prove or disprove without supporting evidence.

If a neighbour is rude to you in the street, because of a dispute over a garden fence, is his aggression motivated by the fact that he is a different colour to you, or does he simply lack self-control? If he uses racially abusive language the issue is simple, but even when excited many prejudiced individuals may find it politic to keep their real objectives private. It generally does not

pay to admit to being a bigot. And there is no reason to assume
that all those who are racially prejudiced will be as lacking in
subtlety as the fire-bombers and manic leafleters. So the problem
remains; without objective evidence, which will often be hard
to get, it is not easy in such instances to be sure of motivation
and of whether or not the incident should be classified as 'racial'.
Your neighbour may be habitually bad-tempered or his temper
may reflect something more sinister.

These difficulties are important because they cause real problems in mixed race areas, especially in inner cities. There are
thousands of small disputes which occur between neighbours in
any crowded urban environment. Any one of these can escalate
if someone suspects that one party to the argument, which osten-
sibly is unconnected with race, has got it in for them because
they dislike their colour.

It is important, then, that people give some thought to how
they present themselves and how they deal with these questions.
This does not mean that individuals need become hyper-sensitive
about race and related issues. Over-awareness of the matter may
be counter-productive. As with questions of gender you can end
up becoming so fixated about it that you project it into everything that happens to you. What is required instead is a little
common-sense forethought and awareness.

1. Those suffering from any kind of racially motivated abuse
should report it immediately. There is now a substantial range
of organizations willing to help people who are in this position,
varying from community groups and local authority agencies to
the Commission for Racial Equality. Other bodies, such as the
police, have become much more conscious of the whole topic,
and sometimes make great efforts to encourage people to report
offences.

2. Anyone who is aware of racial problems occurring in their
neighbourhood, or affecting a friend or colleague, should ensure
that they do something about them. Apart from the gravity of
the matter itself things can escalate out of control, especially in
volatile localities, if they are not rapidly sorted out.

3. Some people will behave in a racist way no matter what happens. Others will be eager to put a racist interpretation on the most innocent statements, gestures or deeds. Individuals at either of these extremes tend to be immune to reason. In a majority of cases, however, sensitivity and foresight will prevent problems.

4. Develop a basic 'feel' for the behavioural and presentational differences between racial groups, in both their subtle and straightforward aspects. Race itself is not the only factor. Age and gender are also significant. In cities West Indian teenage boys may behave much more flamboyantly in the street than their white or Asian counterparts, and the street style of all three groups will differ significantly from that of their parents or their sisters. Behaviour which to one group is threatening may signal nothing more than exuberance to another and so on.

5. Those who cultivate an instinct for these things can save themselves and others a lot of trouble and misunderstanding. A considerable number of street confrontations occur, for instance, because the participants misread each other's intentions. Before they know it the respective parties are pulled into a dispute neither of them wanted.

6. Consult the advice on ways of avoiding trouble in the street.

7. Make a mental list of simple behavioural differences that you observe between groups and individuals whom you encounter. You will be surprised at the extent and nature of some of these variations, even though they will sometimes be hard to detect initially.

8. Consider such differences with respect to your own behaviour. Is it possible that at any time your gestures and bodily mannerisms might be misunderstood by people of a different background? Are you sure that you in turn make the right assessments of others' behaviour?

The aim behind such questioning is not self-censorship. It is pointless if people become needlessly inhibited in case they offend someone. The aim instead is to extend individuals' 'social knowledge' so they can avoid misunderstanding and needless confrontation.

Children

Children are obviously at a severe disadvantage in terms of personal safety. They are smaller, weaker and less experienced than adults. This makes them more vulnerable and their general inexperience means they find it harder to absorb the basic safety rules. Anyone in regular contact with children should therefore try to teach them a certain amount about crime and safety.

However, the tuition must not be overdone. There is very little risk of children being abducted by strangers, for instance, despite the huge publicity that such rare crimes receive (this of course is distinct from cases where children are abducted by parents during custody disputes: these cases appear to be increasing). People under sixteen are at far greater risk from road traffic than from assault or sexual interference by strangers, despite the efforts of certain journalists and campaigners to convince us otherwise. It is very sad that we have reached the stage where children, in broad daylight, are taught to run away from the very sight of unfamiliar men, even on crowded streets. This sort of melodramatic suspicion is totally unnecessary. It also may make it difficult for young people to relate to male authority figures outside home and school, and may be a contributory factor in delinquency and generalized social breakdown.

Perhaps a greater threat than the much-hyped Stranger-Danger is the risk posed to children by people they know, particularly those who insinuate themselves into a child's confidence for sexual purposes. Often such people will abuse positions of trust, as step-parents or babysitters, and they can be of both genders.

It is important, to avoid this, that parents and guardians teach children to talk about their feelings and experiences, so that any such occurrences are revealed (children can be very guilt-ridden and secretive about these things). They should also be warned about the dangers of letting people tamper with them physically. Again care must be taken. Child abuse, despite the hysteria generated in some quarters, is not commonplace. It is socially counter-productive to create an atmosphere in which adults are frightened to have anything to do with children in case their motives are misunderstood, and in which children misinterpret innocent affection.

One advantage of children's vulnerability is that adults are, generally, protective towards them. Even relatively callous individuals will pay attention to a lone child whom they see crying in the street.

Below are examples of the sort of advice children should be given.

1. Very young children, unless they are in the company of parents or guardians, should be taught not to speak with strangers in the street. This advice should be given from an early age, and can be incorporated into games and routine activities, so that it becomes part of a child's world-view.

2. Unaccompanied children should not get into a car with a stranger.

3. If assaulted they should shout and scream and kick hard; they should run towards the nearest area in which other people are present.

4. If they think they are being followed they should not hide in some lonely spot. Instead they should run, as fast as possible, to a shop or to some place where there are lots of people. If all else fails they should go to the front door of any house which seems to be occupied.

5. Each child should know, or have in writing on them, their full name, age or date of birth, and address, plus telephone number.

6. Adults should know:
a. The names and addresses of their children's friends and acquaintances, and their addresses and telephone numbers.
b. Where their children are going whenever they go out (as they get older they should be encouraged to tell their friends).
c. What their tastes and habits are when they are free to please themselves.

7. If your child does a paper round early in the morning ensure that you have checked the route, and that you are satisfied with its safety. Let the paper shop know your concern. Employers have responsibility for the safety of their employees, however little they are paid.

8. Ensure that only you, a member of your immediate family, or another adult nominated by you and known to both the child and the institution, is allowed to collect your young children from school or the play centre.

9. Bullying is often a problem at school. Luckily this is being taken with increasing seriousness by school authorities and social service departments. Find out if your child's school has a properly developed system for dealing with bullies and their victims. If they do not, suggest that they develop one. Do not leave it until your child is picked on. Bullying, with its ambience of distrust and menace, can damage the lives of all pupils in a school, not just those directly affected.

10. Do not put their names or addresses on children's clothing. It simply provides useful information for those who may wish to prey on children.

11. Use common sense when dressing children. It is amazing how some of those who get most heated about child abuse actually dress their own offspring. Parents have the right to dress their children as they wish, but they should consider whether it is always necessary to put young boys in ultra-skimpy shorts simply because it is summer or to let ten-year-old girls wander about in figure-hugging mini skirts. Revealing clothes

can attract those who are interested in children for all the wrong reasons.

12. From an early age children can be taught how to make telephone calls, and how to telephone the emergency services. All children should know the work numbers of their parents and the number of another relative or a neighbour.

13. They should keep small amounts of money so that they can reach home by public transport.

14. They should know how to make a reverse charges call.

15. Do not leave young children alone at home. Plan things so that you make full and reciprocal baby-minding use of neighbours, friends and experienced babysitters.

16. Check the credentials of babysitters who are previously unknown to you. Do not employ anybody about whom you have the slightest doubts. Do not hire anybody as a child-minder who is not registered with the local social services. Inform the police or bodies like the NSPCC if you have doubts about anyone you know who is child-minding. Ring your local council for information about employment of child-minders and about legal controls; when seeking a child-minder ask for the council's list of approved child-minders.

17. Ensure you know your babysitters personally, or at least ensure they come from a reputable agency or obtain substantiated references. With new babysitters it is a good idea, when you are out, to check up on them by telephoning to see if they are actually there looking after your child.

NUISANCE PHONE CALLS

Nuisance telephone calls are a huge problem. Thousands of calls are made every week to and by all sorts of people. And, as in many areas of crime and safety, misleading stereotypes seem to proliferate. The standard image of the nuisance caller is of the grubby misfit in the call box, sweating above his bicycle clips as his stale breath oozes into the receiver. Yet it is not only men, for instance, who make such calls. It is estimated that about 40% of nuisance calls are in fact made by females. Children are also capable of this sort of telephonic harassment.

Nor do all the calls by any means follow the classic grunt-and-groan I Want to Feel You Up pattern depicted in the agony columns. Sometimes an elaborate ritual is enacted before the dirty talk begins. The caller will pretend to have dialled a wrong number, or to be looking for somebody who once lived at the recipient's address. And evidence suggests that in a great many calls it is the victim, not the perpetrator, who does the talking. The telephone rings and is picked up. There is a pause while the recipient repeatedly says 'Hello?', and then there is a click as the telephone is put down at the other end. Of course sometimes silent calls are arbitrary, the result of flawed computer systems, which send electronic signals down the wrong lines. Or people dial the wrong number and are too embarrassed to say so. However, many silent calls, like the more obvious types of telephone harassment, are made by people who know the victim. Perhaps there is an obsession or a grudge is held. Or somebody feels they were the wronged party in a failed love affair.

Whatever the motives, there is no doubt that nuisance calls cause tremendous distress. They can be particularly frightening for elderly or housebound people who live alone. However, recent technological developments mean that there are now more ways of combating the problem than ever before, as outlined below.

1. British Telecom have recently initiated a tracing system. Previously, tracing was difficult and only available in exceptional

cases. Now those receiving regular nuisance calls can apply to have incoming calls tracked to their source. Police intervention and prosecution are then possible if desired. There are technological complexities, but for the vast majority of BT customers the service can be provided with no great difficulty. Exact details of how it works can be obtained by ringing the operator who will then put you through to the appropriate department.

2. BT are also experimenting with telephone receivers that reveal the caller's number. Such facilities are available in other countries, but the obvious benefits must be balanced against the drawbacks. Those calling shops or service centres to make enquiries, for instance, will be effectively giving their telephone number to those bodies, with all the complications that follow when they ring to make an uninvited sales pitch. Opt-out or opt-in alternatives are possible if the scheme is finally adopted nationally, although it remains at the experimental stage.

Obviously, caller-number-identification makes things harder for the perpetrator, but does not guarantee tracing. Harassers may confound attempts at tracing by making brief calls from a variety of call boxes in different locations.

3. Answerphones allow screening. You can hear the message as it arrives and decide whether to pick up the receiver. They also provide taped records of the caller's voice, for later identification. Phones or answerphones that can record conversations in progress are even more useful in this respect.

4. Those worried about calls can go ex-directory. Do not put your number on an answerphone. Sometimes people dial odd numbers at random. If the number is on the tape it helps them to recall it when otherwise they would not have remembered.

Never put your address on an answerphone message. Women living alone might like to pretend on the message that others live with them: 'We are not available at the moment . . .'

5. When you receive a nuisance call there are clear rules of procedure:

a. Do not respond emotionally. An emotional reaction is evidence that you are annoyed or in some way affected by the call, and is what draws many callers into making repeated calls.

b. Put the telephone down immediately once you realize that it is a nuisance call; if it is appropriate say that the call is being traced as you speak or that it is being taped (whether it is or not is for immediate purposes immaterial) – then put the receiver down.

c. Do not give out any information at all, especially any clues as to your address.

6. It is always possible to have your number changed.

7. Interception facilities, for severe cases, are still available from British Telecom, so that all incoming calls are screened, allowing through only those people with whom you wish to talk. This can be arranged by the Nuisance Calls Bureau.

8. Sometimes call recipients are advised to blow a whistle, very loudly, down the telephone line. This is not to be recommended. The harasser may simply do the same the next time they call, and in any case a strong and immediate response of this kind to a call simply confirms that it has made an impact on the victim.

DRUGS AND CRIME
by Rita Goddard

As many as 93% of young offenders are regular drug users, according to a recent survey on drugs and crime, which was discussed at a major conference. The survey provides clear evidence of a connection between drugs and criminal activity. The new survey reveals that although over half of the young offenders interviewed were unemployed they were spending between £150 and £600 on drugs per week, and crime was the primary source of income for the majority.

According to senior police officers who were presenting the findings at a police drugs conference, drugs are responsible for the 'substantial' increase in crime. It is widely accepted that the need to finance expensive drug habits draws people into crime. Many commentators stress that crime is big business and that profits from drug-dealing are used to finance other illegal activities.

There has been much sensationalist reporting about drug misuse. What is really needed is reliable information on drugs. Parents who are worried about drug abuse by their children, in particular, need to know the facts.

The following section has been written with this aim in mind: to provide a non-sensationalist account of the most commonly-used drugs, their effects and the reasons why people are increasingly turning to them.

Case Study: Explosion in Drug Misuse by Rita Goddard

Drug use amongst the young is reaching previously unknown levels, according to the latest research findings of the Institute for the Study of Drug Dependency.

Whilst ten years ago 1 to 2% of school-leavers admitted having tried LSD the 1992 report on Drug Misuse in Britain reveals the figure is now nearer 5%. Use of Ecstasy, unavailable in the UK until the mid-1980s, is on a similar level. Meanwhile, over half a million young people, about 10%, have used amphetamines although cannabis remains the most commonly abused drug in Britain.

These findings show drug abuse to now be a firmly established part of youth culture. Addiction, however, appears to remain relatively low, most young people restricting themselves to 'weekend' recreational use of drugs.

Many youngsters, some no more than thirteen, have been introduced to hallucinogenic drugs at 'raves', all-night parties where drug use is common. Abuse has further spread as former 'niche' drugs, such as 'poppers' (see below or above) and steroids (used for muscle development, and formerly limited to body builders and sportspeople) extends to the mainstream.

Misuse of Drugs
by Rita Goddard

Drugs are a part of most people's daily lives. The drink after work, an occasional cigarette: these are examples of drug use, common to many. However, whilst these substances are associated with very serious health risks, which have been well documented elsewhere and are beyond the scope of this book, both are freely available, legally.

There exists a second body of drugs which are controlled by statute and whose illicit production, distribution or use carries severe penalties. It is these drugs we shall be looking at in this section.

Reasons for Drug Misuse

What makes people, children as well as adults, turn to illegal drugs? It may be one reason, or a combination. Amongst the most common are:

1. The 'danger' element. The thrill of using a substance, knowing it to be illegal, can be a significant part of its attraction.

2. Curiosity. Simply wondering what the effect of a certain drug would be. (If you suspect this is the reason, do not panic. An isolated incident of drug use is not the same as being a habitual user.)

3. Escapism. Both children and adults may find drugs help them escape, temporarily, from an unhappy reality, which may include problems at school or relationship difficulties.

4. Personality problems. An adult or child who is lonely, or lacking in confidence and a sense of self-worth, may turn to drugs for escape and for support in otherwise difficult social situations.

The Tell-Tale Signs

If you are worried that a child or adult whom you know may be abusing drugs there are certain general indicators to look out for. Amongst the most common are:

1. Appetite loss.
2. Uncharacteristic fatigue.
3. Unusual aggression.
4. Inexplicable and sudden mood changes.
5. Erosion of interest in school, work, sport, hobbies, friends.
6. Lying and furtive behaviour.
7. Theft to finance the purchase of drugs.
8. Evidence of stains or smells on the body or clothes, or around the home. You may also find accoutrements of drug use, such as pieces of scorched tin foil or stubs of 'joints' (cannabis cigarettes) with small cardboard filters.

Helping

Naturally, if a child or adult whom you care about appears to be abusing drugs you will wish to help. Understanding the possible causes and being available to discuss the problems is a beginning but you and/or the person concerned may need the help of an outside agency, specializing in supporting those with drug-related difficulties. Please see the Reference Section (p. 259) for details.

The Law

In England and Wales nobody below the age of ten (eight in Scotland) can be convicted of a criminal offence. For those above these ages conviction would depend on the type of drug involved (see below). Normally those under seventeen are dealt with by a juvenile court, in England and Wales. This court is empowered to fine parents or child or order the child to attend an institution. (In Scotland serious offences by children are normally referred to the Reporter of the Children's Hearing.) Allowing one's 'premises' to be used for drug distribution or use is in itself an offence. Thus a parent, friend or partner who allows their home to be used in this way and makes no attempt to stop the activity has themselves offended. There is not, however, any legal obligation to inform the police of suspected drug abuse, although anybody finding what they suspect to be an illegal drug is obliged, by law, to hand it to the police or destroy it.

The 1971 Misuse of Drugs Act prohibits the unauthorized manufacture, trafficking or possession of drugs for non-medical uses. It distinguishes between three categories of drug. Class A, which are judged the most dangerous, carry the highest penalties: life plus a fine for either trafficking or manufacturing; seven years' custodial sentence plus an unlimited fine for possession. Cocaine and hallucinogenic drugs as well as the stronger opioid painkillers are included in this group. Class B, carrying a maximum penalty of five years' imprisonment plus a fine, includes sedatives, cannabis, the more potent synthetic stimulants and the less powerful opioids. Class C drugs carry a three-year sentence and a fine for trafficking or two years plus a fine for possession. Included in this group are tranquillizers and some less powerful stimulants. In practice, however, only some 20% of drug offenders receive custodial sentences or are fined in excess of £50.

The production and distribution of medicinal products is regulated by the Medicines Act, 1968. It stipulates that certain drugs can be supplied only by a pharmacist working from a licensed pharmacy, in accordance with a doctor's prescription. Controls are also imposed on drugs which, whilst not requiring a prescription, may be sold only by a registered pharmacist. The production and distribution of pharmacy medicines, non-prescription drugs which can be sold only by a pharmacist, are also governed by this act.

A Guide to the Main Drugs that are Misused

Amphetamines

Often called 'speed', amphetamines are synthetic stimulants, available medically as tablets or capsules. Legitimate use has included appetite suppression; the drug was also used to enhance the performance of soldiers in World War I. Recreational use became popular among young people in the 1960s, soon leading to restrictions. In recent years amphetamine sulphate powder, which is usually 'snorted' (inhaled), has been the most popular form.

Legal Controls

Most amphetamines are controlled by means of the Misuse of Drugs Act, and all require a prescription, under the Medicines Act. Whilst most amphetamines are Class A drugs, if prepared for injection they then fall into Class B. Some amphetamine substitutes are Class C.

Usage

Amphetamines are widely available and very popular amongst the young, particularly as sulphate powder. Mild usage might be 0.25 gram. High usage could be up to 6 grams a day, depending on the strength.

Physical and Psychological Effects

The nervous system is stimulated, leading to faster breath and pulse rates, the appetite is suppressed and the pupils dilate. Users experience a feeling of heightened confidence, increased alertness and energy.

Hallucination and paranoia can follow heavy, prolonged use; psychosis may also develop. Severe depression, a feeling of lethargy and a ravenous hunger accompany withdrawal.

Cocaine

A strong stimulant, cocaine is similar to amphetamines in its effects. It is a white powder obtained from the cocoa shrub of the South American Andes; the indigenous population are thought to have chewed cocoa leaves as far back as 2500 BC. The practice continues in the plantation districts of South America.

Cocaine was first extracted in 1855, and came to be a widely used stimulant. Up until the turn of the century, Coca Cola contained traces of the drug. During World War I emergency laws outlawing its use were enacted, following unsubstantiated rumours about its use amongst the British forces.

Cocaine is usually 'snorted' through a tube, entering the circulation through the nasal membranes. Less commonly it is dissolved or injected, sometimes combined with heroin.

Powdered cocaine can be chemically processed to alter its structure, producing small hard lumps, known as 'crack'. These are about the size of a raisin and are placed on a piece of tin foil, which is heated, and the vapours are then inhaled. 'Crack' can also be smoked.

Legal Controls

Cocaine, its derivatives and cocoa leaves are Class A drugs. Whilst cocaine is available on prescription, within strict controls, its production, distribution and possession are otherwise prohibited by law.

Usage

Cocaine producers and traffickers have amassed huge fortunes from this expensive drug, whose consumption is often associated with the wealthy. Because of its cost, usage has generally been limited. The popularity of cocaine grew in the 1970s, however, and there is recent evidence of more widespread use.

A regular cocaine user might consume 1–2 grams a day; a 'weekend' sniffer perhaps 0.25 gram over a weekend. 'Crack' users may get through even greater quantities than this, since the effect of 'crack' is less enduring.

Physical and Psychological Effects

Cocaine produces short-term effects similar to those of amphetamines: sensory arousal and a feeling of well-being, with an accompanying depression of appetite and sense of greatly enhanced physical and mental powers. The effect is at its highest between 15 and 30 minutes after sniffing. The effect of 'crack' is much more rapid, since being smoked the drug reaches the brain with greater speed. However, the effect it produces is more short-lived.

Paranoia, anxiety and feelings of severe depression can all accompany intensive cocaine use. When the body has had time to eliminate the drug these symptoms usually disappear. Although less severe than with amphetamines, the after-effects of usage include depression and fatigue. Rarely, overdosing can lead to death from respiratory or heart failure.

Chronic cocaine users are likely to develop a severe psychological dependence which may lead to increased doses. Nonetheless, tolerance or the withdrawal symptoms associated with heroin are not exhibited. The habitual user may, however, experience depression and tiredness if the drug is withdrawn. Smoking the drug may lead to an increased tendency to dependence.

Nausea, weight loss and insomnia are among the negative symptoms that accompany habitual long-term use; a condition similar to paranoia may develop if usage continues. On the whole, the effects do not continue once use of the drug has ceased.

If cocaine is habitually used respiratory problems may develop. Injecting carries its own health risks, including HIV. The membranes lining the nose are damaged by repeated sniffing.

Barbiturates

Since the turn of the century barbiturates have been available in a wide variety of forms. They act as sedatives, which have a calming effect, and, in larger doses, as sleeping pills, such as Nembutal, Seconal and Tuinal. Of all the drugs misused in the UK, these shorter-acting barbiturates are thought to carry the greatest inherent danger. This partly explains why their officially-advised medical usage is limited to the treatment of chronic insomnia.

Most widely available as coloured capsules, barbiturates are also produced in tablet and suppository form. The drug is usually taken orally, although injection may be required for specialized medical treatments. Similarly, recreational users may on occasion inject.

Legal Controls

Under the Medicines Act unauthorized supply of barbiturates is an offence, although possession is not. Permitting premises to be used for the distribution or manufacture of barbiturates is also illegal. The drug is legally available only from a licensed pharmacist on production of a doctor's prescription.

Usage

The increase in heroin use, the stricter legal restraints on barbiturates and the more general availability of tranquillisers and sleeping pills (see below) have led to a considerable reduction in the misuse of the drug. Twenty, or even ten, years ago, it was widely available to would-be recreational users.

As a result of thefts from factories or pharmacists some barbiturates find their way on to the illicit market, as do some drugs which were originally obtained on prescription.

Physical and Psychological Effects

Barbiturates work in the same way as alcohol, depressing the central nervous system. The effects usually last for 3–6 hours. A small dose, one or two pills, generally induces a feeling of relaxation and good-humoured sociability, similar to the effect of one or two alcoholic drinks. However, on occasion a feeling of anxiety, hostility or depression may be experienced.

Poor co-ordination and slurred speech may be observed in the user who has taken a moderate to large dose. There may be mental confusion and extreme emotional reactions, followed by sleep.

Accidental overdosing on barbiturates is not difficult, since there is a very fine line between the normal dose and what could prove to be a lethal one. For this reason, respiratory failure leading to death, following overdose, is a real danger amongst prescribed and recreational users. The risk increases if barbiturate consumption has been accompanied by the use of alcohol or other depressants.

As with other drugs, injection produces the most rapid effects. All the possible negative effects of barbiturates are greatly increased by this form of administration, including the risk of overdose. Skin abscesses, as well as gangrene and HIV, are other related dangers. Barbiturate injection may be the most dangerous form of drug use.

Heavy use of barbiturates may lead to hypothermia, bronchitis and pneumonia, as well as a pattern of accidental overdose. Whilst normal prescribed doses should not produce serious physical dependence, higher dosage can produce chronic withdrawal symptoms of a severe nature. These may include very low blood pressure, hallucinations and fits.

Opiates, Opioids, Narcotic Analgesics, Including Heroin

Use of opiates was widespread in the nineteenth century, when they were freely available without prescription from grocers' shops and similar outlets. They were used to cure numerous ailments, as well as for recreational purposes. 1868 saw the introduction of legal controls on opiates, as a result of increasing awareness of the risks of dependence and poisoning combined with fears that their use by working people might divert them from their labour. Britain, in accord with an international agreement, restricted opium and opiates to medical use. The drug has remained available on prescription to those dependent on it.

Addiction spread in the 1960s with younger users trafficking supplies obtained on prescription from a small number of GPs. As a result, in 1968 stricter controls were imposed and permission to prescribe heroin became limited to a few specialists. A considerable black market in imported, illegally produced heroin began to grow in the mid-1970s and the use of opiates has continued to grow significantly. Because of its relative potency, smuggling of even small amounts of heroin is considered a worthwhile risk.

Whilst opiate powders can be swallowed or dissolved in water and injected, heroin is not usually swallowed, since this has minimal effect. Users tend to sniff heroin or smoke it; in the latter case heroin powder is warmed and the fumes it gives off inhaled, often through a small tube. This process is called 'chasing the dragon'. Pure opium can be either eaten or smoked. It is possible to make some opiate mixtures non-injectable by dissolving the powder in certain substances, which is one of the reasons why opiate addicts are often prescribed methadone mixture.

Legal Controls

Opiates are strictly controlled under the Misuse of Drugs Act. Possession without a prescription is illegal, as are the unauthorized supplying, production or distribution of the drugs. Allowing premises to be used for their manufacture is similarly illegal. Those who are dependent may obtain heroin and dipipanone (a synthetic opiate normally used as a painkiller) from a licensed doctor, although other opiates are available in the normal way on prescription.

'Synthetic opiates', methadone, dipipanone, and pethidine, together with morphine, heroin and opium, are Class A drugs, under the Misuse of Drugs Act. Class B drugs include codeine and dihydrocodeine, which become Class A if prepared for injection. Buprenorphine and dextropropoxyphene are categorized as Class C. Medicines to treat coughs or diarrhoea which contain very dilute mixtures of morphine, opium or codeine are not controlled and are freely available at chemists' shops.

Usage

There are believed to be over 100,000 regular and heavy opiate users in Britain, although only about one-fifth are registered addicts. Registration means a sufferer is treated by a specially licensed doctor, who notifies the Home Office of the patient's addiction. Addicts usually inject the drug. Recreational use of the drug has recently developed among teenagers, who frequently 'snort' it. Meanwhile, in 1988 almost half of the new addicts registered were under twenty-five. Some people become dependent on synthetic opiates, often illegally obtained.

The rise in heroin addiction is linked to its increased

availability. Since the 1970s growing amounts of the drug have been smuggled into Britain: 331 kilograms were intercepted by customs officers in 1989. As the supply has increased so the price has fallen, although dealers are nonetheless likely to adulterate the drug with substances that have the same physical appearance as heroin, such as talcum powder or glucose.

Physical and Psychological Effects

Whilst novices may feel nauseous and vomit, habitual users claim opiates induce a feeling of pleasant drowsiness and euphoria. Although the functioning of the nervous system is depressed, motor skills, intellect and sensation are little affected. Overdose can lead to stupor and coma, whilst death due to respiratory failure is a possible risk.

If heroin is injected, the substances used to dilute it can prove harmful, even fatal. However, injection is popular, since it gives the greatest and quickest effect.

Tolerance develops amongst regular users, whose health often deteriorates through inadequate nutrition. Constipation may become a problem, together with loss of interest in food, as well as in sex.

As tolerance develops users are likely to increase their dose, and heroin sniffers and smokers may move on to injecting the drug. The physiological effect of heroin is such, however, that overdosing, which as we have seen can be fatal, is only likely when a user takes what was their normal dose after a sufficiently long period of abstention for their former tolerance to have faded.

Withdrawal, whilst not dangerous, can be very distressing, the former user exhibiting symptoms similar to severe flu or cramps, which last about a week. A strong psychological craving is much more likely than a physical addiction and some people are able to limit their intake to occasional recreational use.

When unadulterated, opiates are relatively safe drugs and notified addicts who maintain a healthy, stable life-style should not suffer serious physical consequences. Babies born to opiate users tend, however, to have a lower than average birth weight and may be born suffering withdrawal symptoms. Illegal users of opiates, the most commonly injected misused drug in Britain, are in the high-risk bracket for HIV.

LSD

LSD – lysergic acid diethylamide – first produced in 1938, is derived from ergot, a fungus, which is found growing wild on certain types of grass. The first trip was taken, for experimental purposes, by a scientist, Albert Hoffmann, who also discovered the drug, in April 1943. During the 1950s and '60s the drug came to be used for the treatment of psychotic patients. LSD went on to be used from the 1960s as a recreational drug in the US and then in Britain, some users claiming LSD to be a path to transcendental experiences. The British government reacted in 1966 by controlling LSD under the Misuse of Drugs Act; medical use virtually ended within the next two years.

LSD is a white powder, generally combined with other substances, taken in the form of tablets or in solution, or absorbed into blotting paper, sugar cubes or gelatine sheets. The use of other synthetic hallucinogens, like PCP (phencyclidine) and the hallucinogenic amphetamines (for example MDA), is very limited in Britain, except for Ecstasy (see below).

Legal Controls

The Misuse of Drugs Act categorizes LSD and other strong hallucinogens as Class A drugs, and their use, for medical as well as non-medical purposes, is strictly controlled. Only those who are licensed by the Home Office, for example in the course of approved research, may handle these drugs. Unauthorized manufacture, supply and possession are illegal. Allowing one's premises to be used for the production or trafficking of these drugs is also an offence.

Usage

There has been a relatively low incidence of detected offences involving LSD although this may well, at least in part, be explained by the drug's peculiar qualities – simplicity of manufacture and minute dosage. Nonetheless, LSD use is not wide-spread. Although there is no recent research, it is estimated that probably no more than 1% of the population, overall, have used LSD, primarily in their youth. Usage amongst students is considered to be significantly higher, at 3–8%.

Although in the '60s and '70s use of LSD was seen as a 'mind-expanding' experience, associated with the more uncon-ventional amongst the young, it has since been more widely adopted, many users being more interested in taking the drug for recreational purposes.

Dosage is small; as little as one microdot can produce a halluc-inogenic experience, or 'trip'.

Physical and Psychological Effects

A 'trip' generally lasts about 12 hours. Its character can vary enormously and tends to depend upon the user's mood and the environment. Generally, in the more well-adjusted, a trip may induce feelings of increased awareness or a belief that one is having a mystical experience; the senses become heightened, colour and sound intensify dramatically. An unstable or depressed user of the drug may experience anxiety or depression. LSD may, indeed, trigger a psychotic experience amongst users psychologically predisposed to mental illness, although this is most often as a result of repeated usage.

There are no other risks known to be attributable to LSD: earlier fears that repeated use could cause damage to future children appear to have been misplaced.

Users do not become physically dependent on the drug, to which a tolerance quickly develops, so that abstention between doses becomes necessary. Psychological dependence on LSD affects only a small proportion of users.

Cannabis

The cannabis plant, *Cannabis sativa*, grows wild in many parts of the world. Resin, formed into blocks, 'hashish' or 'hash', provides the strongest form of the drug; herbal cannabis, 'mari-juana' or 'grass', is less potent. The first documented use of cannabis is as a herbal remedy in ancient China and until 1973 the drug was available in the UK on prescription, although its non-medical use has been banned since 1928. The popularity of the drug in the UK, which began to develop in the '50s and '60s, originally stems from the 'beat/jazz' culture of the '50s and usage amongst immigrant groups. The drug is usually smoked, in the form of 'joints', cigarettes comprising a combination of tobacco and cannabis.

Legal Controls

The Misuse of Drugs Act prohibits both medical and non-medical use of cannabis. Herbal cannabis, resin and oil are Class B drugs, whilst chemical derivatives of the plant, which are very unusual, would be Class A. It is an offence to grow the cannabis plant, produce the drug for use, supply or possess it, unless authorized by the Home Office. Allowing one's premises to be used for the production or supply of cannabis is illegal, as is allowing one's premises to be used for smoking it.

Usage

Cannabis is the most widely used of illegal drugs: it is the subject of 80–90% of all drug seizures. Smoking cannabis appears to be a leisure activity amongst a significant cross-section of young people. A 1982 survey, for England and Wales, found that 5% of those aged sixteen and above admitted having used cannabis, many within the last year. The actual figures may, of course, be much higher. Recent usage was most common amongst men and women below thirty, particularly those who had completed further education. Heavy, regular users are likely to smoke five cannabis cigarettes, 'joints', daily.

In recent years, increasing numbers of users have been obtaining the drug from 'home-grown' plants, which are relatively easy to cultivate in Britain, both indoors and outside. Nonetheless, cannabis used in the UK is primarily obtained from the Middle East, North Africa and Asia.

Physical and Psychological Effects

As with LSD, effects relate to the user's mood and the situation in which the drug is taken. Whilst novice users may find the effects limited and vague, the drug usually induces a feeling of relaxation, a tendency to laugh, and talkativeness. Heightened sensory awareness is another effect, similar to that induced by LSD but of lesser intensity. Concentration is adversely affected – driving skills, for example, would be impaired. Feeling hungry is common and anxiety may be felt, particularly by less experienced users.

Confusion may accompany high dosage and heavy users with latent or existing psychological disorders may find their condition exacerbated. Again, this is similar to LSD. There is no real risk of overdosing.

Cannabis is relatively quick-acting and the effects may last several hours, if the dosage is high. At the end of the experience the user will feel tired. Cannabis can also be drunk or eaten, producing a longer-lasting effect, but since the dose cannot be regulated any unpleasant feeling the drug may induce would be more difficult to avoid. Users do not become physically dependent, although mild withdrawal symptoms may be experienced. A psychological dependence may, however, develop.

Regular smoking of cannabis 'joints', combining cannabis and tobacco, can bring similar health problems to those associated with smoking conventional cigarettes. Respiratory problems, for example bronchitis, can be brought on by cannabis use and there may also be a link with lung cancer. Foetal development may be adversely affected by heavy cannabis use and the drug may encourage premature birth. Recently, there have been claims by some MS sufferers that use of cannabis helps relieve their symptoms.

Despite the fear that cannabis use may lead to experimentation with 'hard' drugs, such as heroin, there is no evidence of a direct link. In recent years there has been considerable debate on the question of legalizing cannabis.

Ecstasy

Also known as 'E' or 'XTC', Ecstasy, which is a hallucinogenic amphetamine, produces effects which combine those of amphetamines and LSD. First produced in 1914, the drug is derived from oils of natural products, such as nutmeg.

Legal Controls

Ecstasy has been a Class A drug since 1977, following an amendment to the Misuse of Drugs Act. It may not be prescribed by a doctor nor may it be used for research purposes without a Home Office licence.

Usage

Sold in tablet form, Ecstasy has been available in the UK since the mid-1980s. Its popularity has grown since 1988 with the rise of Acid House parties or 'raves'. Use has since spread to young people not connected with the Acid House party scene.

Physical and Psychological Effects

Ecstasy is a relatively slow-acting drug, and the effect of a single dose may last several hours. The pupils dilate; nausea, a dry mouth and throat, and loss of appetite are usually experienced. Co-ordination may be impaired, making driving potentially dangerous. The subsequent 'come-down' may be similar to that experienced by amphetamine users, with its characteristic feeling of fatigue and depression.

In a similar way to LSD, the nature of the user's experience depends on mood and surroundings, whilst expectations also play a part. An initial 'rush' of euphoria is followed by a feeling of calmness and the dissipation of anger. Orgasm in both sexes and erection in men may be inhibited. Heightened, non-hallucinogenic, perception is experienced, although at high dose levels these may become hallucinogenic. Negative experiences, where higher doses have been taken regularly, such as panic, confusion and psychosis, have been reported.

There is some speculation that the drug may adversely affect the immune system, since susceptibility to minor ailments is increased in the long-term user. Whilst tolerance does develop, physical dependency does not.

For those who suffer from high blood pressure, heart disease, epilepsy or glaucoma, or who are in generally poor physical or mental health, the drug seems to carry particular risks: women with genito-urinary tract problems should similarly avoid its use. No foetal or neo-natal effects have been recorded. Some Ecstasy-related deaths have been reported; although the exact link between the drug and the cause of death is unclear.

Alkyl Nitrites

These drugs come in two forms: amyl and butyl nitrite, known as 'poppers'. Similar in chemical structure, both are clear yellow fluids, which are inhaled. For medical use amyl nitrite is produced in the form of a small glass capsule encased by cotton wool. The user releases the drug by crushing the top of the capsule with his fingers – producing a 'popping' sound. Alkyl nitrites available illicitly come in small phials with plug or screw tops.

Medical usage of alkyl nitrite, to help relieve the chest pains of angina sufferers, began shortly after its discovery in 1857. Recreational use of the drug, primarily for its believed aphrodisiac qualities, was first seen in the 1930s. However, the roots of its current popularity lie with the US gay community, who began using the drug in the 1960s on discovering its value as a muscle relaxant, facilitating anal intercourse. In 1969 anxiety over abuse of the drug in the US led to its categorization as a prescription-only drug.

Butyl nitrite is available in the US as an air freshener, free of the legal restrictions on amyl nitrite; its primary market continues to be the gay community.

Legal Controls

The Medicines Act categorizes amyl nitrite as a pharmacy medicine, allowing it to be supplied by a chemist without prescription. In practice, however, since it been supplanted by more efficacious drugs, its medicinal availability is low. Meanwhile butyl nitrite, not controlled by law, is more widely obtainable. The question has been raised of regulating alkyl nitrites under the Misuse of Drugs Act, although to date they remain outside its control: the courts may seek to invoke other legislation, such as the Offences Against the Person Act 1861, to limit the drugs' street availability.

Usage

As in the US, use of these drugs in Britain, particularly butyl nitrite because of its freedom from control, is greatest amongst the gay community. Some 'English poppers', thought to be amyl nitrite, are available here. Most easily obtainable, at outlets which include pubs, clubs and sex shops, is butyl nitrite, imported from the US and sold under brand names such as 'Rush', 'Ram' and 'TNT'.

It is the male gay community which continues to be the main user of alkyl nitrites, although the linkage of the drug with Aids (see below) is thought to account for a fall in use amongst this group.

Physical and Psychological Effects

On inhalation, the effects of these drugs are immediate, lasting 2–5 minutes: the heartbeat races, blood vessels dilate and there is a rush of blood to the brain. Users profess the drugs heighten and prolong sexual pleasure: they are known to relax the anal sphincter, facilitating anal intercourse.

The sudden drop in blood pressure which accompanies inhalation of the drugs could lead to unconsciousness and even heart attacks, and although no fatalities have been recorded to date those with heart conditions should not indulge in their use. Pressure within the eye increases, so the drugs could also be particularly harmful to glaucoma sufferers. A feeling of debility and headaches, sometimes accompanied by vomiting, are other, common, side effects which are exacerbated if the alkyl nitrites are used as part of a drug 'cocktail'. Accidental spillage on the skin produces a painful burning feeling. The skin of the nose,

cheeks and upper lip may be affected by nitrite dermatitis, sometimes accompanied by swelling and pain of the nasal passages,
similar to sinusitis. This will clear within about ten days providing use of the drug is not resumed. Methaemoglobinemia may
result from excessive usage: sometimes the lips and skin become
tinged with blue, and sufferers can experience vomiting, shock
and may become unconscious. Death may result in extreme
cases, when the drug has been swallowed.

Users do not appear to exhibit psychological dependence or
withdrawal symptoms. However, within 2–3 weeks of repeated
use tolerance builds up. This is lost after a few days' abstinence,
the user being especially prone to headaches if use is resumed.

Since they are rapidly expelled by the body, alkyl nitrites do
not appear to have long-term consequences for healthy adult
users. Nonetheless, Kaposi's sarcoma, a form of skin cancer and
one of the earliest symptoms of Aids, has been linked to usage
of these drugs.

Case Study: Problem Family
by Glen Warren

Carol sits curled up in the armchair. Her eyes flit around the
room, never stopping long enough to focus on anything. Rubbing her arms as if cold, scratching the inside of her forearms,
she drums her fingers on the arm of the chair. These aren't signs
of nerves, but of withdrawal. She hasn't had a fix for a day or
so.

She's not always been like this, with her lank and brittle dyed
blonde hair, like wet straw. She looks much older than her
forty-one years. Once she was slim, lithe and beautiful. Everybody said so. She could have been a model.

Puberty came early, giving her a well-developed figure before
any of her friends. It attracted first the older boys, then the men.
She began to get invited to parties, and went to as many as she
could. She was always getting chatted up. Carol loved that,
thought it was great fun. Eventually one smooth-talking man,

Steve, succeeded. He chatted her up, took her to his flat, and made love to her. Carol admired his worldliness. He was twenty-four.

It was the most glorious experience, the best feeling in the world. They continued to see each other, making love every time they met. Her parents didn't like Steve; there were lots of rows over her seeing him. They tried to stop her, but had lost any control over her: she was sixteen and could do what she liked, she said. She left home and moved in with Steve.

One night he persuaded her to smoke a joint, saying it would improve their love-making. It had. The sex was better than ever. Carol became a regular smoker, but it used to make her sleepy. They would smoke a joint, have fantastic sex, and she would nod off. Steve gave her some pills to combat this, adding that it would make the sex even better – and that she would keep awake to enjoy more of it. And he was right. Gradually, he got her on to more and more drugs – different kinds and increased doses, until life was a blur. In the mornings she couldn't remember the sex any more, just the lingering of immense pleasure. And the desire for more.

Steve began to tire of Carol. He started staying out all night, giving flimsy excuses even Carol could see through. When, six months into the relationship, she didn't see or hear from him for four days and nights, she left.

She signed on. She was lucky and found a small flat. She knew she ought to try and find a job, but all she really wanted to do was satisfy her craving for drugs. Finding a dealer, but having very little money, she offered herself in payment. So she went from taking drugs to have sex, to having sex to get drugs. And she's still doing it. Over the years the drugs have ruined her looks. Now she is known throughout the local area and beyond. If you have a bit of blow in your pocket, and fancy a shag, go round to Carol's, that's what the blokes say. All drugs welcome. The more dope, the longer you're welcome. If you have smack or coke, she'll be your slave for as long as it lasts. If she can, she'll try to get money out of you as well – promising to pay it back, but with no intention of doing so. Her visitors have ended up coming mostly from the filthy end of society – dirty old men to whom she is the only means of gratifying their lust; men who haven't washed for months, whom you can smell from fifty yards off. All count Carol as a good poke.

During this downward spiral, she has had three children. The eldest, Kevin, was a good little boy, but as he got older, he become wayward. It started when Carol couldn't be bothered to go and get her own drugs; she would send Kevin. He would sit around the dealer's, smoking dope. He was only eleven, but the dealer didn't care. Then Kevin started to cut a little bit off for his own use, stealing from his mother. She went mad when she found out. She never sent him to score for her again.

Having acquired the habit, Kevin had to find a means of paying for it. He turned to crime, working his way up from shoplifting, through mugging, into burglary, and then doing building societies and banks. As he moved up the ladder, he became more interested in crime than drugs. He still likes a blow now and again, still pops pills, and occasionally has a trip, but it is now a hobby. His real interest is crime. It's his job. He likes the pay, for such little work.

He is currently serving a twelve-year jail sentence for armed robbery and assaulting a police officer.

Next is Gerald. Carol doesn't like him. He took over the drugs scoring from Kevin. Although he liked a smoke, he quickly realized the money to be made out of drugs. After a little time spent gaining the dealer's confidence, Gerald approached him with a deal. A while later Gerald left with a quarter of an ounce of cannabis resin to sell at school. In two days it was gone, and he was back for more. He has been a dealer ever since. It's the only 'job' he's ever had, and it's got him a lot of money. He has risen through the ranks of dealership to the point where he is now a supplier to the street dealers. He has a BMW, all the latest in hi-fi and television equipment, expensive suits, a model for a girlfriend – she looks just right on his arm – the whole 'young executive' bit. No one suspects he lives in a council flat in Hackney, and signs on the dole every Thursday.

It's not the flashy life-style that's made Carol dislike him – nor the fact that Gerald passes on none of his wealth to her. She could handle that. Nor is it the damage he has done to people's lives, pushing drugs at them. That doesn't bother her at all. What really upsets her is that he made her pay for her drugs, up-front, like everyone else. When he started making a living at it, she saw herself being set up for life, free drugs whenever she wanted. She was furious, she was his mother, she promised to pay when she had the money – wasn't his mother's promise good enough? The answer was no. Gerald knew that if he gave in once, he would have to do it all the time, and he would never get the money.

The youngest child, also a son, is Tony. He is basically honest, but not very bright. This got him into lots of trouble when he was younger. His elder brothers would put the blame on him when one of their schemes went wrong, and he used to get punished severely for things that were not his fault. He was put in care after being found in possession of a can of petrol and a lighter, after his brothers had failed to burn down a school and dumped the evidence on him when making their get-away. Then he went to a young offenders' centre after Gerald gave him a toy as a gift while still in the shop. As soon as Tony passed through the door, he was arrested for shoplifting. But not once has he put the blame on his brothers. Always he has tried to stick by his principles. He is slow, but determined. As soon as he could, he found himself a job on a building site, and got a flat. That's what he's still doing, leading an honest life.

Carol is not keen on Tony. She feels he hasn't tried to make anything of his life. Not like Kevin and Gerald.

USEFUL ORGANIZATIONS

The Suzy Lamplugh Trust

The Trust was established late in 1986 after Suzy Lamplugh disappeared without trace, earlier that year, whilst going about her work as an estate agent. She has never been found. The Trust's initial concern was to raise awareness of violence and aggression, and it is now the leading national charity dealing with the subject of personal security, teaching people to 'live their lives to the full, without fear'. The Trust is particularly active in education and training. It organizes numerous projects and programmes and is always eager to develop new ideas and initiatives. Many of its most prominent products and activities are listed below.

Published Works

Beating Aggression,
by Diana Lamplugh,
Weidenfeld and Nicolson (1988)
Without Fear,
by Diana Lamplugh
Weidenfield and Nicolson (1991)

Research

'The risks in going to work: the nature of people's work, the risks they encounter and the incidence of sexual harassment, physical attack and threatening behaviour,' London School of Economics and Political Science (March 1989).
'Relative risks of taxi and minicab', research by Dr John Groeger (1991), which led to the setting up of a government working party.

Booklets Written and Published, with Assistance, by the Trust

Reducing the Risk (on personal safety) Funded by BT.
A Guide to Safe Travel Funded by Cellnet.
Travel Safely by Public Transport Funded by Dept of Transport, reprinted by British Transport Police.
The Trust's *Acorn Magazines*.

Training Manuals Published by the Trust

Suzy Lamplugh Trust Training Manual (1989)
'Well Safe' Education Pack for 14–16-year-olds, with Barbara Pagan (1991)
Personal Safety: Training Resource Manual, with Chris Cardy, Gower Publications Ltd (1992)

Talks

Full-time schedule of talks and training throughout the country for all kinds of organizations, by Diana Lamplugh.

Conferences and Conference Reports Available from the Trust

'Aggression and Violence in the work-place', London University, 1988
'Aggression and Vulnerability at Work': Conference, University of London, 1988.
Working with the Sex Offender', 1990
'Sentencing of Sex Offenders', 1991
'Missing Persons – Whose Responsibility?', 1992

Government Committees on which the Trust is Represented

Health and Safety Executive's Committee on Violence.
Department of Transport, Working Party on Minicabs.
HSE Committee on Violence, Financial Sector.

Other Projects and Achievements

'Avoiding Danger': video to raise awareness of work-place aggression, giving practical advice. October 1987, available from the Trust.
Personal alarm commissioned.
Missing Persons Helpline launched 1989.
June 1992: Diana Lamplugh awarded an OBE in the Queen's Birthday Honours for her work with the Suzy Lamplugh Trust.

Victim Support

Victim Support schemes operate across the country. They offer guidance and support to crime victims.
 The initial British Victim Support group was established in

Bristol in 1974. They grew rapidly in popularity and within a few years the National Association of Victim Support Schemes was established. Since 1987 the Home Office has provided funding for local Victim Support activity and the projects function in their hundreds, throughout England, Scotland and Wales.

Volunteers receive training and the schemes have become increasingly sophisticated and ambitious.

Police refer people to schemes on a local basis and will provide advice and information for those who want to help, or who need help themselves. Contact details, for those who wish to get in touch with the Victim Support national office, are available in the reference section of this book.

4. Home Security

The Public

Burglary's public impact resembles that of car crime. Huge numbers are affected by it. The number has grown, over the past decade, while the incidence of recorded burglary has swelled dramatically. The mortgage culture of the 1980s also means that even more people own their homes than before. Ownership of property, as opposed to its rental, means that people cannot walk away from their homes and problems. They often cannot simply move out of burglary-ridden areas.

From one viewpoint it is ironic that the same recession that killed the property market, trapping people in high-crime areas, has also encouraged the criminality that threatens houses. This opinion is based on the idea that many burglars are youthful products of the underclass which has expanded because of the damage to the economy.

Perhaps a contributory factor is the comparative failure of Neighbourhood Watch (defeating burglary was one of the main objectives of the watch concept). Maybe this failure is due, despite the enduring popularity of watch schemes, to other failures of resourcing and implementation: these are complicated questions. Additionally it can be argued that watches have not failed, that in fact property crime would have gone even higher without them. It is hard to prove this one way or another.

Yet the practical issue remains. Despite its awareness of the scale of the problem, the public, paradoxically, remains under-motivated about the basic techniques of preventing burglary. Those in authority need to take major steps to counteract this.

The Criminals

Burglars come largely from the same underclass that produces car thieves. In fact they are often the same people. They tend to be very young and to be only casual attenders at school or work. Many of them are unlikely, unless things change dramatically, to have any stable career or educational prospects at all. They often grow up in restless, noisy environments without the constant presence of a father figure. All these things show in their personal mannerisms: a slightly ominous playfulness, a fidgety and abrasive sense of humour. Talking with them you are impressed by their aimlessness, but this can suddenly be replaced, in the middle of the conversation, by a sharp-edged perceptiveness.

They have a clear idea, for the most part, of their prospects. They know the police have only a slim chance of apprehending them, and they are unimpressed by what the courts might visit upon them if they are actually caught. This hard-headedness is allied, paradoxically, to a style of operation that is arbitrary and casual. They like to practise burglary in or near their home areas. For all their arrogance they are uncomfortable in environments they do not know well and their approach to housebreaking can be quite whimsical and 'impressionistic'. If they dislike the 'feel' of a property they are capable of abandoning a perfectly straightforward burglary whilst actually on the premises.

But their emotional, spontaneous approach does not mean that they are incapable of planning and calculation. They are capable of considerable foresight on occasion and may work in teams of two or three. It takes nerve to go 'cold' into a strange house, and the presence of allies provides comfort and practical assistance and helps with planning or preparation. They usually watch a property first, and prefer to avoid houses that look adequately secured. One thing which makes them hard to detect and track is that they are a mixture of attributes: impulsiveness and calculation, adventurousness and timidity.

Yet there is a small minority of burglars who display a very different crime profile. These are a bit older and more experienced. They are not interested in ordinary targets and are prepared to go long distances to get into suitable dwellings. They are specialist and skilled housebreakers, in pursuit of high-quality antiques and paintings. They are no threat to the ordinary householder, but obviously cause real problems for the affluent.

What currently unites these different types of burglar, and what should most worry the public, is their general invulnerability. Very few of them are caught and the punishments they receive, if prosecuted, do not seem to deter many of them from reoffending.

Much of the impending restructuring of the police service, and of the criminal justice system, is motivated by an awareness of the wholesale failure to do anything about these offenders. A big test of the reforms, in the long term, will be their impact on burglars.

The Police

Burglary, like car crime, remains a major embarrassment for most police forces. They have simply been unable to stop it from rising hugely over the past decade. 'It's one of our biggest headaches,' one senior officer remarked. 'There's a feeling . . . within the ranks that it's out of our control.'

Over the years a great deal of police energy has gone into attempting to solve the problem. Numerous initiatives have been mounted, from publicity campaigns to the establishment of Neighbourhood Watches. None of them has made any large-scale difference.

Some police officers, as with car crime, think that the matter is beyond their control. A typical comment is: 'Increased reporting of crime . . . the recession and youth unemployment. Those are the roots of it. Perhaps when the recession ends it will tail off a bit.'

Yet the pressure, as long as burglary continues as a big issue, remains on the police. The drastic reorganization of the police service, which is highly likely to be undertaken in the near future, may for a while absorb any surplus police energy. The public might have to wait until after that process before it can look to the police for fresh thinking about burglary (with the exception of projects like Operation Bumblebee, profiled below).

Case Study: Operation Bumblebee

'We are at war with burglars . . . We will make it clear that anyone doing burglaries or dealing with burglars will be severely dealt with . . .' These words, spoken by a senior police officer, indicate a new approach to burglary which is being pioneered by the Metropolitan Police. For a long time it has been tacitly accepted, by police and public, that there was not much law enforcement agencies could do to catch burglars. The burglary clear-up rate was almost legendary for its lowness.

But now, after burglary has reached record levels, with house-hold insurance payments rocketing to cover the thefts, a more dramatic approach has been attempted by the Met. Dawn raids, by officers with warrants, are mounted on the homes of teenage housebreakers and their accomplices, after weeks of surveillance and careful collation of 'information received'. Huge amounts of property are recovered in the process. In one raid, for instance, thirty-four people were arrested at fifty-two homes across North London; police recovered thousands of pounds worth of stolen jewellery, silver, cable TV equipment, videos and stereos. Police are convinced that the initiative, entitled Operation Bumblebee, is part of the answer to the burglary problem. They claim that burglary figures in targeted areas show a considerable decline. Other forces are following the Met's activities with interest.

Police, however, are still bitter at what they see as the social and legal changes which make it more likely that adolescents will commit burglary, and which mean that often they receive paltry punishments if they are caught and prosecuted. Committing property crime is no longer viewed as being particularly wrong in many sectors of society, they say. One officer, commenting on the burglary upsurge, said: 'It has come about because some years ago society took the approach of going for the soft option, giving one chance after another to people who were getting away with it with impunity. If the courts had not been so soft then, we would not be seeing the results of it now. Somewhere we have totally turned the moral tide . . .' Bumblebee is a powerful contrast to what has become the standard police approach to burglary (see the immediately preceding section on policing and home security). Its activism and optimism directly oppose police fatalism and disinterest as regards this issue. It will be interesting to see if Bumblebee's sense of energy and initiative inspires other police forces.

The Government

The government is even more embarrassed by the burglary figures than everybody else. After all, the Conservative Party took office with the promise of doing something about law and order, a traditional Tory issue. Nearly fifteen years later we find that burglary, along with many other offences, is reaching record levels. All the rhetoric, all the extra resources poured into policing have been for nothing. The position is so bad that the Labour Party has begun to steal some of the Conservatives' law and order platform for itself. In attacking a government as inept as the present one the burglary figures have been of great assistance to the political opposition.

Conservative anger at these humiliations has focused on the police, once the Tories' ally. There is a sense of betrayal: 'We throw money and resources at the boys in blue. And how do they reward us? They reward us by letting property crime, not to mention a lot of other crime, go through the roof,' said a senior Conservative.

For the general public much depends on whether the Tories are happy to blame the police alone. The government is likely to take a close and sceptical look at all aspects of current criminal justice and not just policing, from the organization of courts to the provision of high-quality research, there could be significant changes. Certainly the government, with its appalling recent record, is under huge pressure in all areas of life. A drive against inefficiency in criminal justice might seem like a good way of regaining support. The danger for the government is that if it fails, like previous Conservative law enforcement efforts, it could make things even worse for it than at present. And the Labour Party, with its new law and order policies, will sustain the parliamentary pressure. Law and order may become an even bigger political issue as the next election approaches. The burglary problem will probably take up a large part of that debate.

Industry and Commerce

The manufacture and fitting of security devices, ranging from alarms to floodlights, has long been big business. Householders pay large sums for such mechanisms and they have a wide range to choose from. The price and quality vary enormously: some are of a very high standard and are reasonably priced, others are both expensive and inefficient. Sound alarms are notorious for going off by mistake – to the enormous irritation of the police, who spend much time and effort answering false calls.

The structure of the industry itself is also the target of criticism. One expert comments: 'Security firms work in an *ad hoc* way. The industry has grown up piecemeal and things are not properly geared to the way that the public and the police think about home security. Certain of the products are superb. Others are dire. But what is needed is a coherent approach, with a proper wide-scale assessment of the market need. What you've got at the moment is the opposite: just fragmented competition between different firms without any clear perspective.'

Another major way in which industry and commerce are involved in home security is through sponsorship. The recession has limited this to some extent, but it still continues and will expand again when the recession lifts. Mostly sponsorship means backing official crime prevention schemes or those mounted by voluntary groups. Insurance companies and specialist security firms, in particular, back a wide spread of such initiatives. Neighbourhood Watches are eager for sponsorship, as are groups, like Crime Concern, which are charged with inspiring and supporting general crime prevention.

The position at the moment, as regards home security and the private sector, is exceptionally confusing. This is mainly because of the muddle and inconsistency emanating from Whitehall and its agencies. Nonetheless it seems reasonable to assume, as far as the ordinary consumer is concerned, that the government will attempt to pressure the security industry into voluntarily regulating standards, for the improvement of overall quality. This has especial relevance for sound alarms, as mentioned above. The need to conform to comparatively decentralized, free-market methods makes such standardization even more complex. The government will continue to encourage private investment in home security and crime prevention, though it will be some time before the full impact of such things is felt by householders. Of course, such policies are liable to sudden and arbitrary change, and must be regarded as provisional until the very last moment before implementation.

The Media

Home security has a relatively poor media image. With a few significant exceptions the emphasis is on the problems and the risks. Partly this is because it is difficult to interest journalists in such a seemingly tame and mundane subject. And so when they do write about it they tend to rely, as a substitute for real thought, on a stock of vague presuppositions. Attempts to fight burglary, especially when they take a community and preventive approach, are therefore often portrayed as being well-intentioned but naff or as covert vigilantism.

However there are signs of change. Police and related organizations in the field are becoming more proficient in their public relations. As a result home security issues are presented to the media in a more lively style. Also it is possible that burglary has become so prevalent that people, inside and outside the media, are forced to think more carefully about what it means and the importance of its prevention.

Nonetheless, the current media stance towards home security remains largely uninspiring, despite these signs of change. For the public this may have severe consequences. Home security needs to be presented to them positively. If it is not then far too many houses will remain soft targets for burglars. A sustained effort is required to change the way that the whole subject is put across to the public.

Research

A considerable amount of academic research is conducted into topics involving home security. Quite often this research tends to examine the issue in relation to larger questions about communities and police and social structures. Research that closely examines the specific mechanics of house security seems rarer than that which looks at these broad issues. Interdisciplinary research, encompassing technological, administrative and sociological approaches, does not seem very widespread. It is an obvious line of future development.

A problem for the public is that much academic research, in this subject, is published in a form that is not easily accessible. It is not widely distributed, nor easily understood by the non-specialist. Wider and clearer dissemination of research results would benefit both the public and the universities.

Commercial and industrial research, in contrast to university activity, tends to have a relentlessly nuts-and-bolts approach. Where much university research is perhaps too theoretical, the opposite can be true of work undertaken directly by industry and commerce.

The public might gain considerably, and much burglary might be foiled, if the theoretical consistency of academic research were successfully married to the hard-headedness of industrial and commercial organization. There are signs already that such collaboration is being attempted. Much depends on how universities cope with the massive changes government has forced on them in the last few years.

Case Study: School Break-in
by Rita Goddard

This book concerns itself mainly with domestic burglary. Nonetheless it is useful to reflect on the massive amount of damage caused by burglary of public premises. At some schools, for instance, burglary is a regular occurrence, as the piece below describes.

Trails of yellow and red powder paint bend across the floor of Class 1. Coloured pencils are scattered everywhere. A small cage lies empty. Its former occupant, a gerbil called Jeremy, is missing.

For the class teacher, Mike Grant, facing a vandalized classroom has become almost a Monday morning routine. Looking around to see what else has been damaged, he notices that the children's Diwali collage, in celebration of an Asian festival, has been ripped apart. Reference books have been thrown around but none are missing. Thieves tend not to be great readers, Mike muses. They would have been much more interested in the video and the computer, but these are safely locked away behind a heavy door. Despite several previous attempts they have so far been unable to get to them. Mike Grant is sure that they will try again, but what most disturbs him is the thought of the lesson, in the workings of the world, that the children will get when they arrive. They adored the gerbil, and spent hours grooming and feeding him.

Next door, in Class 2, Ms Rajni Amin, Mike's colleague, clears some debris from the floor. She is relieved that the aquarium has not been touched and that the murals, carefully painted by her pupils, are still intact. But the collection of foreign coins, representing the ten different nationalities of the children's parents, has gone. She will spend some time picking up torn work-sheets and erasing the race-hate slogans that have been daubed across the walls. But compared to previous occasions Class 2 has, in her words, 'got off pretty lightly'.

For Classes 1 and 2 of St Ignatius Primary School this is the third break-in this half-term. Ironically it is only a week or so since the head grandly announced, during assembly, that plans were afoot to install sophisticated security devices, plus new and stronger locks on doors and windows. No longer would the school be an Arcadia for burglars. Privately the teachers have severe doubts as to whether any of these proposals will be implemented. There is always somebody somewhere, amongst the multitude of committees that regulate school life, who wants to veto new developments because of their cost. The fact that proper security might prevent huge repair bills makes little difference to those who enjoy playing games in committee meetings. The small children in the care of Mr Grant and Ms Amin can, for the immediate future, look forward to some nasty Monday mornings.

HOME SECURITY: PRECAUTIONS AND FITMENTS

General Precautions

Time, noise, visibility: these are what the burglar dreads. Anything which increases the time needed to gain entry, and which makes the thief more visible or audible, will discourage and hinder him either before or after an attempt upon someone's home.

It is important, for deterrence, to give an impression of activity. Burglars are put off if they get the feeling that the house is well maintained by people who are alert, streetwise and often at home.

The following precautions should be noted.

1. Hedges and Fences

High hedges and fences camouflage burglars while they are tampering with doors and windows. Cut hedges low and trim them regularly. The same applies to other external foliage, such as shrubs and bushes. Fences too should be low. The security benefits compensate for the fact that the house may look a little less cosy and appealing.

2. Drain Pipes

The space between a drain pipe and its wall should be filled in with cement. This especially applies to the solid, old-fashioned pipes which give a good grip. Such action makes it hard for the burglar to get a solid climbing hold on the pipe.

Anti-climb paint is easily applied to drain pipes and walls. Again this makes it difficult for the burglar to get a grip. The paint sticks to clothing and helps identify intruders. Put up warning signs or stickers. These deter thieves and prevent accidental damage to the clothing of innocent parties.

3. Dustbins

Burglars can climb dustbins to reach windows or low flat roofs. Keep bins away from the house itself. Some police officers suggest that bins should be chained to the property's perimeter wall. (Ensure they are unfastened when the dustmen arrive.)

4. Vital Signs

Unused milk bottles at the front door; newspapers protruding from letter boxes; unopened mail on the hall mat, visible through the letter box or glass; all these things tell the aspirant thief that the property is empty and that the departed occupants have little sense of security. Anyone going away for more than a day should cancel newspaper and milk deliveries and should arrange for mail to be collected or rerouted.

Other signs of an unoccupied house are untrimmed lawns and

dry drains. Again neighbours or friends can trim grass or run the taps briefly every few days.

5. Stickers

Even if there is no dog, a 'Beware of the Dog' sign, prominently positioned, is a useful deterrent. People have been known to put a food bowl and kennel in the garden, as part of the deception. Neighbourhood Watch and property-marking stickers are useful in the same way.

6. Hiding Places

Burglars are highly aware of the usual hiding places for keys. Most people put them in the same old places, imagining that they are being extremely ingenious. Never hide keys outside a property. Do not put them on a string through the letter box, nor under a mat or flower pot or piece of garden statuary, nor in the bottom of a hedge. Neighbours and friends can be entrusted with a spare key and this is by far the safest option.

7. Key-holders

Those installing burglar alarms are expected to provide police with the name and address of an additional key-holder.

8. General Fitments

a. Security Bars

Sometimes people fit metal bars or grilles in front of, or behind, doors and windows. Usually they are lockable. They are extremely strong and it is very difficult for burglars to penetrate them. The two main drawbacks are appearance and fire safety. Bars do not look good and people often dislike 'living like a prisoner'. Escape in a fire may also be problematical, especially if the keys cannot easily be found. Householders should carefully assess the advantages and disadvantages before fitting bars, preferably in consultation with a crime prevention officer. Bars should only be locked when the house is unoccupied.

b. Safes

Do not keep cash at home, except in a safe. The best type of safe is set in concrete and concealed beneath the floor. In a flat, except for a ground-floor flat, this will not normally be possible and a properly hidden wall safe is required. A bank safe deposit box is cheaper, though less convenient, than a home safe.

c. Security Lighting

Lighting has two main security functions. One of them is deterrence. Most burglars are uninterested in houses which seem occupied because there is plenty of light. The second is visibility: burglars hate being seen by potential witnesses or interveners.

(i) Internal Lighting

When the house is empty lights should be left on. Leave the curtains partly open, so that the light is evident but the minimum is revealed about the house interior. Do not simply leave the hall lights on. This convinces nobody that anyone is in: people do not live in their hallways. It is wise to leave several room lights on, on different floors. Lavatories and bathrooms are the best rooms to leave lit, in case burglars check on occupancy by calling at the door. Inexpensive timer switches may be used. They will operate the lights at different times, helping to sustain the illusion of occupation. Timer switches are even more useful if the house is empty for a prolonged period.

Leaving lights on does not cost a great deal in electricity. It costs even less if the newer, low-consumption bulbs are used. These are more expensive to buy, but in the long term are far cheaper. They need as little as a quarter of the electricity of a normal bulb, and they last about eight times longer, whilst providing the same amount of light.

(ii) External Lighting

Porch lights make it hard for a burglar to operate unobserved, and they make door callers of all types highly visible. Lights can additionally be fitted at other points which might shelter intruders, especially in the front or back garden.

Timers or light-sensitive switches ensure regularity of operation, and floodlighting systems are frequently triggered in the same way as noise alarms. Indeed they are often installed as back-up to a noise alarm system. Infra-red detectors, for instance, activate light in response to body heat, and the light remains as long as the heat source and/or for a set time after the heat source departs.

9. Noise Deterrence

The noise of a radio, tape, television, or other audio device deters potential intruders. Timer switches can be used.

10. Dogs

Do not keep dogs solely for security. A large and vicious animal can cause chaos in a small household. However, an animal which is part of the family, and is well cared for, may be a useful deterrent, provided other security measures are taken as well. Dogs that bark all the time are not very helpful. Nobody will pay close attention if they bark because of intruders.

11. Garages and Sheds

Lock away implements used for DIY, otherwise a burglar may employ them in getting in. Ladders, especially, must not be accessible. Secure them in sheds or garages, or fasten them to a wall.

Case Study: Architectural Liaison

One enlightened attempt, by police and other crime prevention agencies, to deal with burglary is described by the term 'architectural liaison'. What it amounts to is co-operation between architects, home builders and police to incorporate crime prevention measures at the design stage of house-building. Instead of trying to fit security devices afterwards, when perhaps burglars have already paid a visit, the concept relies on planning and co-ordination to make it very hard indeed for burglars to have anything to do with a particular property.

Estate Design

Estates should be put together in a style that emphasizes the sense of community and neighbourhood, and they should have definite boundaries, which are clearly marked. Lighting must be adequate and parked cars should be visible. Architecture should balance the desire for privacy with the need to avoid creating landscape hiding places for criminals. Above all, the prospective thief should feel exposed and at risk of detection when he enters the estate.

Physical Security

This involves fitting basic but comprehensive security. There must be good locks on doors and windows, points of entry must be secure and properly put together. The general layout and maintenance of the house must make it as hard as possible for intruders to operate.

Intruder Devices

Proper lighting and good alarm installations, conforming to high standards, are also required. Systems are fitted in consultation with police and care is taken to ensure that fitments are of the best available quality.

Those interested in the concept should contact local police to see if a scheme operates in their area. The details of schemes will vary considerably from area to area.

Doors

External Doors

The strength and solidity of the door itself are its most important security features. It is pointless putting really good locks on a door so weak it can be easily kicked or battered through. Wooden doors, provided they are solid, have an advantage over other types because they are more adaptable, especially when fitting locks and other security devices. The wood should be at least 44 mm thick, and should definitely not be of 'eggbox', plywood or chipboard construction.

Aluminium or UPVC doors should have in-built security devices. These doors are very hard to modify.

Glass and wood panelling, strutting and other refinements weaken a door and make it easier to force.

It is very hard to penetrate steel doors, steel-reinforced frames, and metal gates and grilles in front of doors. Although these are more secure than wooden doors, they are also more expensive, can present a fire hazard, and are of less attractive appearance. Many people dislike the 'prison-like' ugliness of a very heavily secured door. Householders must consider these factors when establishing the appropriate balance between security, expense, aesthetic considerations and fire escape.

Internal Doors

Do not lock internal doors when going out. Burglars, when inside a house, know that noise and visibility are less of a problem than when outside. In their haste they will smash any obstructive internal doors and locked cupboards and drawers as well. Locking internal doors and cupboards only makes it likely, therefore, that they will be badly damaged. However, internal doors should be closed whenever possible. This stops fire spreading, especially at night, and could save lives.

Door Locks and Fitments

All locks should conform to British Standards specifications. The identifying kite mark should be displayed on all purchased locks (see the section on British Standards).

1. Levers and Tumblers

Keys work, when inserted into a lock, by operating levers or tumblers. The more levers or tumblers there are the harder it is to pick the lock or to fashion a duplicate key. A mortice lock should therefore have at least five levers to prevent any possible picking of the lock.

2. Mortice Locks

A mortice lock fits *into*, rather than on to, a door. This type of lock is, therefore, much harder to remove, or to tamper with, than other kinds. The bolts, to stop them being sawn through, should have internal reinforcing bars.

Some mortice locks have added handles and latches. They are useful for doors, such as back garden doors, which are securely locked at certain times, but which at other times must be opened frequently without constant locking and unlocking. Usually the handle operates a simple latch bolt which, separate from the mortice bolt, slots into the door jamb and keeps the door shut but unlocked. Mortice locks need careful installation. If incorrectly installed they may severely weaken a door.

3. Rim Locks

A rim lock is usually mounted on the door surface (on the 'rim'). It is easier to fit than a mortice lock but also easier to remove or neutralize.

4. Deadlocks

A deadlock is a lock which can only be opened by a key or by force. Its bolts can only be moved back into the lock by the action of a key. A thief cannot, therefore, reach in and open the door from outside, without a key, and the lock cannot be slipped with a plastic card. It can be operated by a key from inside or outside.

5. Push-Button Combination Locks

Combination locks, either electronic or mechanical, function when numbered buttons are pressed in a particular sequence. They are especially suited to those who frequently lose keys or to groups of people who regularly use the same door. Key copies are not needed and numbers may be changed at will. However, thieves may discover the combination numbers. It is therefore important not to be seen punching in a combination number and, if possible, it should not be written down. If the number must be recorded it should be disguised, perhaps as a fax or telephone number, or in a simple code.

6. Surface Bolts

These are quite easily fitted on the inside of a door. They slide open and are therefore no fire risk. They are often used by women who are at home alone. Simplicity is their great merit: they can be pushed into place quickly and without much effort. Their weakness is the ease with which an intruder can open them once he gets in, or if he reaches through broken window glass.

7. Padlocks

Padlocks are often used on outhouses or garden sheds. Many spring-loaded padlocks are easily levered open. However, a close shackle padlock, both opened and closed by a key, is much more secure. Usually it cannot be levered open because there is not enough of a gap in the padlock to force or lever it open, and it is very difficult to saw through. Generally speaking padlocks should always be fitted with a bar (a 'padbar').

8. Keys

The following basic points apply to all key-operated security devices.

a. If possible take all keys with you on leaving home.

b. If thieves cannot find keys, after they enter, then they are often forced to leave the way they came in. This obviously can reduce the size and amount of material they are able to take.

c. It is always dangerous to deadlock yourself into a house. Mortice locks should not be used when at home, nor the dead-locking action on a rim lock. There is very little chance of burglary whilst a house is occupied. At such times fire is a bigger risk than burglary. A door chain, plus surface bolts top and bottom, are the best option for those who feel insecure whilst at home, and present minimal fire risk.

d. Those moving into new premises should have the locks changed. It is always difficult to know who, amongst previous occupants or visitors, may have copies of keys.

9. Outward-Opening Hinge Bolts

For outward-opening doors. These bolts make it difficult to force open the hinge side of the door (by forcing out the hinge pins) and they lock into a strengthened hole in the door frame when shut.

10. Rack Bolts

Positioned on the lock side of the door, these are morticed in. The key operates only from the 'hallside'.

11. Frame Bar

Also known as the 'London bar', this is a steel bar fixed on the inside lock side of the door frame. It strengthens the rim lock 'keep' on the frame and also supports any accompanying mortice lock.

12. Door Chain

This allows the occupant to communicate with those outside without giving full access. The chain is even more secure if longer screws are fitted than those supplied with the chain. Use of a chain gives the occupant 'thinking time' with which to assess those outside.

13. Door Viewers

There are two main types.

a. Lens Viewer

This is a small lens which resembles a miniature telescope. It fits into the door and usually gives a wide-angle view of those outside. Often the lens is of the 'fish-eye' type, which allows a 180-degree field of vision. It is normally installed in the centre of the door.

b. Mirror Viewer

This is a compact two-way mirror set in the door centre. The occupant can see through the mirror and move it to one side, to talk to the visitor, while the door stays shut. Small documents may be put through the narrow aperture. When not in use a strong metal shutter shields the device.

Both types of viewer should, preferably, be installed by those experienced in such work. Viewers are of course useless at night, unless a porch or hall light illuminates those outside. Such lights can be operated internally, or automatically by such devices as passive infra-red detectors, so that the light activates if someone approaches.

14. Entryphones

Audio, or closed-circuit television, entryphones are increasingly popular. However, cameras may easily be neutralized and voice-only entryphones can be deceptive. Entryphones are a supplement, and not an alternative, to more conventional security devices.

External Doors: Specific Requirements

The different security requirements of particular doors are considered below, regarding the locks and other devices described above.

1. Front Doors

Panelling, strutting and glass, as mentioned earlier, should be minimal: these weaken the structure and also allow the burglar to reach through. Wood panelling may be strengthened by nailing reinforcement wood on to it with clutch-head or non-reversible screws or Phillips screws with defaced heads. As in all security matters, it is best to seek a balance and to avoid extremes.

The following specifications will provide reasonable security for a front door, without incurring great expense, unreasonable fire risk or damage to the appearance of a property.

a. A frame bar fitted down the lock side of the frame.
b. A rim deadlock fitted to the upper part of the door.
c. A five-lever mortice deadlock positioned about a third of the way up from the bottom of the door.
d. A spyhole in the door centre, at a comfortable height.
e. A chain at an easily reached level, but preferably half-way between the two locks.
f. All front doors should have at least three hinges.

2. Back Doors

Many of those who take care with their front door are surprisingly lax about their back door. Often back doors are of poor quality wood. The best option is to buy a strong front door and use it as a back door. As always, the door should have minimal glazing and panelling. Sometimes people like back doors to admit plenty of light. In this case small or narrow panes, with strong strutting, are recommended.

Back doors have their own usage pattern. People do not like locking or unlocking them every time they enter or leave the back garden. The most practical security equipment for such a door is rack bolts at the top and bottom, plus a five-lever mortice sash lock (a sash lock is a lock with a handle) in the middle. When the door is in constant use, and people are frequently moving to and from the garden, the sash lock may be used without the mortice. When the house is empty, the mortice and bolts can be used.

3. Patio Doors

The phrase 'patio door' is sometimes used vaguely, but often means a sliding door, and this is how the term is used here. Such doors, which frequently have glass panelling, attract burglars because they can be lifted out of their frames, especially with the help of a lever. This is often because of the space left above the door installation. This can be sealed with wooden 'battening' (wooden strips). Tools, especially forks and spades, should not be left nearby, as thieves may use them in gaining entry.

A hook and bolt style of lock may be effective, and is similar to a mortice lock. Surface-mounted locks should be installed at the top and bottom of the doors.

Difficulties may be encountered with metal or plastic patio doors. Often only surface-mounted locks can easily be fitted (it is hard to drill mortice cavities in metal or plastic.) Expert fitting is advised.

If patio doors are bought as part of a double glazing deal it is worth checking, carefully, that guarantees are not adversely affected by alterations. Many modern patio doors have in-built anti-theft and multi-locking devices. Look for these when you buy them.

4. Outward-Opening Doors with External Hinges

Outward-opening doors are more resistant to external force than inward-opening doors. Their weakness is their external hinge pins which can be driven out. These can be protected by hinge bolts at the top and bottom.

5. Double Doors

Double doors, including french windows, need two mortice security bolts (rack bolts), installed vertically top and bottom, on each door. In the centre should be a good quality five lever sash lock. If french windows open out you need hinge bolts.

Windows

A great many casual burglars get in through windows that are left open or unlocked. Windows should never be left open, and locks should always be activated, when a house is left empty, even for short periods.

The sight of window locks actually in use vastly reduces the casual burglar's interest, for penetrating properly secured windows heightens the risk. Getting in takes longer, is noisier, and is more likely to draw attention. The burglar knows he cannot follow the normal procedure of breaking a small piece of window glass before reaching in and unfastening the catch. The window will simply not open without a key. Breaking a lot of glass is noisy, fragments of glass fly everywhere, and jagged and dangerous shards have to be negotiated or removed. If the window locks are combined with other home security fitments, such as good door locks, the casual burglar will often find his attention drawn towards easier targets.

Two key-operated locks should therefore be fitted to each downstairs window, and to each upstairs window that adjoins flat roofs, high walls, drain pipes, and any other architectural features that give access.

Do not give burglars a good view of room contents. Net curtains, shutters and venetian blinds help in this regard. They need not be fully drawn, and thieves are more likely to think people are in if curtains are partly open.

Locks and Fitments

Wooden Frames

Wooden window frames are generally preferable to those made of plastic, aluminium, or other non-wood substances. This is because wooden frames are relatively easy to fit with locks or to modify in other respects.

Non-Wooden Frames

Specialist skills are normally required in fitting locks to plastic or metal frames, but even this tends to be unsatisfactory. It is best to ensure, when you buy them, that all non-wood windows are already fitted with two locks per window. Where possible such windows should be of tubular material, as this makes adaptation easier. Metal windows require self-tapping screws that are strongly fixed.

Locks should be simple and straightforward in operation, otherwise they may be wasted: people anxious to get out in the morning are reluctant to fiddle with time-consuming locking systems. Locks which take time to screw into place are inferior, in this respect. Perhaps the most convenient type of window lock is the 'snap lock', which can be snapped shut without a key, but needs a key for opening. Push-button locks are often similar.

There are many different window locks. Most of them, however, are variants on the same locking methods. The following examples give an idea of the range available.

1. Hinged Wooden Windows

a. Window Press Bolt

The bolt is mounted on the opening frame and locks when it is pushed into place on the lock plate, which is set on the fixed frame. Opened only with a key, this is useful for side, top-hinged and various pivotal windows.

b. Casement Window Snap Lock

The bolt is on the opening frame, and fits into the lock plate on the fixed frame, locking automatically when the window is shut. It is released only by a key.

c. Lockable Window Handle

The lock plate is mounted on the handle, while the bolt is on the fixed frame. It locks automatically when the window shuts, but opens only with a key.

2. Sash Windows (Sliding windows)

a. Sash Window Press Bolt

A spring bolt is pushed into place, locking the two frames. A key is required for release. This lock needs window frames that are level when shut, as it is mounted on top of the frames.

b. Sash Window Bolt

A bolt locks both frames and is key-operated. This is a very simple and solid locking mechanism and makes little difference to the window's appearance. It is also suited to frames that are not very level. A disadvantage is that the key takes quite a long time to lock or unlock the bolt. Two should be used for each window.

3. DIY Locks

Wooden frame windows are quite easily secured on a do-it-yourself basis, especially as a temporary measure. Frames can simply be nailed down. Some householders do this with particularly vulnerable front and rear windows. On a sash window a hole can be drilled through the inner and outer frames, so that a screw may be inserted. Such drastic measures should only be taken after careful thought, and at least one adjacent window should always be openable, as a fire escape route and for ventilation.

Some small 'transom' or 'top-hinged' windows are probably best nailed down permanently. Many burglars are young, compact and agile and may use such windows to reach or climb through. Always confer with a local police crime prevention officer before nailing any windows.

4. Louvre Windows

Louvre windows have overlapping glass slats and resemble venetian blinds both in appearance and action. The glass sections fit over each other like roof slates. Burglars are fond of louvres because they are so easily levered from their frames. No really good locking device has yet been developed for such windows. Internal bars, or temporary gluing, are perhaps the only remedy. Many security specialists recommend replacement with other types of window.

Glass and Home Security
by Bert Dady, Metropolitan Police

Glass has an important role in home security, but is comparatively neglected as a subject. Below, the security aspects of different types of glass are examined in turn.

Float Glass

This is the most common type of glass in domestic use. It breaks easily, but makes a great deal of noise and leaves jagged splinters which must be removed to gain entry. This obviously makes life hard for burglars. Float glass is relatively cheap and easily installed. It is clear and looks pleasant.

Wired Glass (Squared Wire Inside)

This is *not* a security glass, but a 'fire' glass. It is harder to break than float glass, but when broken it crumbles into granular particles and the whole pane can be easily pushed out. There is little noise or danger of the intruder cutting himself. In my opinion it is less effective against burglary than float glass.

Toughened Glass

Such glass, which is mostly used in vehicles, gymnasiums and doors, is actually pre-stressed float glass. Four to six times stronger than ordinary float glass, it offers good protection against blunt objects, but is very sensitive to blows from hard, pointed instruments. When finally broken the whole pane crumbles into granular particles, as noted above. There is very little risk of injury for a burglar.

Laminated Glass

Laminated glass consists of a sandwich of two sheets of ordinary glass permanently bonded with a plastic inner layer. On impact the glass breaks but the pieces adhere to the interlayer which is very difficult for a burglar to penetrate. A great many blows are needed to break through a properly fitted sheet of laminated glass. It is not particularly affected by sharp objects or punches. Most domestic burglaries are effected through windows, so it is worth considering fitting laminated glass.

Burglar Alarms

Intruders, as we mention elsewhere, worry about time, noise and visibility. Too much of any of these, whilst a crime is proceeding, will bring them into contact with the police and the courts.

Burglar alarms encapsulate all these problems for a thief. Alarms can trigger shattering noise levels and flashing lights, both of which attract attention; they may be directly linked to security alert centres; attempting to neutralize them takes time and may in any case be futile and further increase the risk of attracting attention.

For these reasons a visible alarm system deters casual burglars. It represents both an actual barrier, because of the difficulty of surmounting it, and a symbolic barrier, because it indicates that the householders are security-conscious and may have taken a wide range of precautions against theft. Alarm systems should, therefore, be visible (some people even put fake alarm boxes on the front of their house). The sounder box, the part that makes the noise, should be prominently placed on the outside wall of the property.

The big problem with most alarm systems is that they tend to go off accidentally. More than 90% of all burglar alarm activations are 'false activations'. This truly astonishing failure rate means a lot of wasted time and vastly reduced effectiveness: police and neighbours are less likely to respond because of this fact. Indeed police will refuse to answer a particular alarm that they know has frequently gone off by mistake.

On top of everything else, false activations cause a great deal of annoyance, especially late at night when people are trying to sleep. Many alarms, partly because of this, carry a strobe light fixed to the sounder box. The noise is set to stop after a reasonable interval, but the light will continue working, after the sound has stopped, until the alarm is reset.

The risk of false activation reduces if alarms are installed and mounted by those skilled in such work. Shop around carefully before purchasing such equipment. Local crime prevention officers will give impartial advice on the matter. Buyers should also check, before purchase, that alarm systems conform to British Standards (p. 25).

Burglar Alarms: Basic Functions and Equipment

A burglar alarm should perform four basic tasks:

1. It should detect intruders.

2. It should vigorously raise the alarm.

3. It should be easy to switch on and off.

4. It should, as mentioned above, be visible enough to deter.

An alarm system should consist of:

1. A control unit.

2. The detection equipment itself.

3. The sounder box, with its siren or bell and flashing lights.

4. A battery which supplies power in the event of power failure.

5. Internal sirens to disorientate a burglar who is inside the house and is disregarding the noise of the main alarm.

How Burglar Alarms Work

The strengths and weaknesses of a particular system are governed by several crucial factors, as outlined below.

1. Operational Suitability

Different alarm systems are designed for different tasks. Everything depends on the particular nature of the property being defended. Householders should think carefully about their exact requirements, so that they choose the equipment most suited to their own needs.

2. Control

Some control units are more sophisticated than others, allowing the user to activate all or parts of the system as required. Simplicity is vital: the controls should be easy to understand and to operate.

3. Circuits

Alarms are governed by electronic circuits and most of these work in a similar way.

a. Closed Circuits

These sound the alarm when the circuit is broken after the 'detecting' device (see below) responds to an intruder within the system's area of operation.

b. Open Circuits

The alarm sounds when the circuit is completed, via a detector device's response to an intruder.

c. Non-Wire Systems

The detection devices transmit warning signals to the control unit, which then sounds the alarm.

4. Detection Devices

These are the 'switches' or 'triggers' which react to stimuli and raise the alarm. As one police officer put it, 'If the control unit is like a military command centre, then the detector devices themselves are the forward observation units which make initial contact with the enemy.' A wide choice of such mechanisms is available. Below we give some examples.

a. Pressure Mats

Pressure mats set off alarms when people stand on them. Usually they are hidden under carpets or mats, often near doors or windows. A problem is that, after a while, the shape of the mat can be seen through the previously concealing surface. Children or animals, furthermore, can trigger them accidentally.

b. Vibration Detectors

These are attached to window glass, window frames and doors. They respond to small movements, such as light blows on a door or window. Beware false activation. Sometimes, if there is heavy traffic nearby, or a strong wind, they need adjustment to stop them going off needlessly.

c. Magnetic Reeds

These devices are installed on or in doors and windows. Some are set into the body of the window or door, although others are surface-mounted. When the door or window is opened the circuit is broken and the alarm is triggered.

d. Passive Infra-Red Movement Detectors

An intruder's radiated heat is what causes such mechanisms to activate the alarm. Often they are wall-mounted, in a hall or a main room and are sensitive to radiated heat variations. They sense sudden changes in such heat and need specialist and careful installation to avoid false activation. Many things can set them off accidentally, from strong sunlight to domestic pets.

e. Ultrasonic Detectors

Usually these mechanisms are attached to the wall of a room. High frequency sound waves, which humans cannot hear, are transmitted and are received again by the transmitter when they bounce off the room's hard surfaces. Someone entering the room alters the frequency of 'reflected' sound and the alarm then goes off.

f. Sound Detectors

There are portable sound detectors which can be moved from room to room. Because the sensors in the device will respond to loud and/or sudden noises, they can be triggered by harmless street noises or parties underway nearby. However, the most advanced versions of these detectors can be programmed to respond only to certain specific noises, and they can often 'tell' the difference between the sound of a smashed window and a falling bottle.

g. Radar Detectors

Such a device resembles a miniature radar station. High frequency microwave radio signals detect movement in the system's vicinity. The alarm is then triggered. The microwaves cause no known damage to the human body.

5. Non-Wire Alarm Systems

Such systems are more portable and easier to fit than most of their wired counterparts. They are easily transported and installation requires none of the drilling and nailing needed with wired mechanisms. They are not as reliable as 'hard wire' systems.

There is a central control mechanism which processes radio waves that connect it to detection devices. Control is kept through a pocket-sized box that can be used in any part of the house concerned.

6. Telephone Alarms

Alarm systems which connect to a telephone should use a telephone line which is 'outgoing only'. Lines should enter premises as unobtrusively as possible, preferably underground.

One example of such a system functions when a coded telephone message, on an 'outgoing only' telephone line, is transmitted to a 24-hour monitoring station. There the message is automatically decoded. The staff, who are normally working from a security company's HQ, then inform the police. A variety of signals can be transmitted, for example, 'intrusion' or 'fire'. The message can be relayed up to twenty times, if there is no response, to ensure it reaches its target.

Buying an Alarm System

Always follow the precautions outlined below. By so doing you may save yourself a huge amount of time and trouble.

1. Never buy a system from a door-to-door caller.

2. Choose reputable dealers.

3. Ensure that all purchased equipment conforms to British Standards (see the section on British Standards).

4. Check whether dealers belong to reputable trade organizations, such as the NSCIA (National Supervisory Council for Intruder Alarms), the BSIA (British Security Industry Association) or the IAAI (Inspectors of Approved Alarm Installers).

Not all good security firms belong to these bodies. There are excellent companies which belong to no professional organizations. However, those who do belong to such groups are bound by certain professional standards in their dealings with customers, including the client's right of redress for substandard work or service. Good firms who are outside these bodies may be significantly cheaper, but may not offer the redress and regulatory facilities that are so important. Individual purchasers should balance these differing factors for themselves.

5. Find out whether your insurer reduces your house contents premium if an alarm system is installed. This is more likely if the security company belongs to one of the trade organizations mentioned above.

6. Always compare prices before money is exchanged. Prices can vary markedly from company to company. Electronics-based industries, because of the pace of research and development, change rapidly both in costings and in technology. So ensure your price information is up to date and comprehensive.

7. Look carefully at agreement terms, even if they are with a highly regarded company. Maintenance terms are crucial. Particular attention should be given to the details. Sometimes people end up paying large amounts over many years without receiving much in return. If in doubt get professional advice, *before* you sign any agreements.

8. Houses vary as much as people. Different dwellings have different security requirements. A security company must visit the home concerned before undertaking a major installation, otherwise they cannot assess the appropriate security requirements. There should be no charge for assessment visits.

9. After installation, the inhabitants should not have the problem of negotiating trailing wires and cables. These should be out of sight, making it harder for burglars to tamper with them.

10. Always confer, before buying any system, with your local crime prevention officer.

DIY Alarms

There are various alternatives to the expensive business of purchasing an alarm system that is fitted by a specialist company. Most of these involve installing the equipment yourself or via cheap but competent local labour.

The do-it-yourself option has two main drawbacks. One is that it may reduce insurance eligibility or increase insurance costs. The other is the greater risk of sub-standard installation, which can be both dangerous and counter-productive. Damage to the wiring can cause fires or serious electrical shock, and those who fit systems that do not work will not necessarily know this, falsely imagining that they have made themselves more secure. Only those who are reasonably versed in the required skills should attempt to fit electronic security systems.

Many systems can be bought through mail order. Yet not all instruction manuals and leaflets would win prizes for plain English. Decoding instructional documents can deplete large reserves of time and temper and cause some of the problems mentioned above.

A lot of difficulties are bypassed if a local electrician or fitter installs a system bought from a reputable dealer. This is cheaper than installation by a big company but may be comparable, or even superior, in quality. Remember, of course, the comments made above about the need for redress if things go wrong.

The newest and most sophisticated technology, however, such as passive infra-red detection, will probably require specialist installation. The more sensitive the equipment is, the more carefully it should be installed.

If equipment is fitted by a non-specialist company or individual then it is even more vital that, beforehand, advice is taken from the nearest crime prevention officer. And extra careful attention should be paid to the relevant British Standards.

Property Marking

Property which carries the owner's identifying details deters and compromises burglars. Items marked with names, addresses, post codes and similar details are hard to sell. They can also be easily traced, making it more likely that the thief or 'receiver' will be caught. Householders, whenever possible, should mark portable valuables and place stickers on the items, declaring that they have been marked.

Marking additionally makes recovery easier for the owner of the goods. Many stolen items which have been recovered stay in police storage, simply because nobody knows where they should be returned.

Crime prevention officers will advise about the best marking methods. Frequently a post code is used, along with the house number. If the address alters then an x is placed next to the original mark and the new details are added. Detailed post codes are to be found in local directories, or in public libraries. Alternatively you can telephone the Post Office post code information service.

You can buy comprehensive property-marking kits, providing equipment for most types of marking, at a low price in many outlets. Alternatively crime prevention officers or watch co-ordinators may lend marking equipment. Think carefully, in each case about whether the marks should be visible or 'invisible' (see below).

Get the owner's consent before marking rented or borrowed items.

Methods

Visible Marking

Both ceramic and diamond-tipped markers are widely used. Either can etch a car's registration number on its windows, but otherwise they have different applications. Ceramic markers are best for vitreous enamel, glass, china or any hard glazed surface. A metal compound makes the permanent mark and does not scratch or cut the surface. Usually a stencil is provided. Harder materials, such as polished wood, plastic, gold, silver and other metals are best marked with diamond-tipped engravers.

Antiques

Antiques may lose value if marked, although sometimes value increases because items are more easily traced. Antique dealers and other experts will advise.

Stamping

Heavy tools and machines, including bicycles, drills and lawn mowers, are stamped with a quarter-inch die and a hammer. A set of letters and numbers is used.

Electrical Engravers

Hard surfaces can be marked with electronically driven engraving devices.

Invisible Marking

Invisible marking is often done with pens that resemble felt tip pens. The ink is ultra-violet and the marks are only visible under strong ultra-violet light. The advantage is that damage to the appearance of valuables is limited. The disadvantage is that it is not permanent, and strong rubbing and polishing may weaken the marking.

Obviously many valuable items, such as jewellery, antiques, documents or fabrics, are difficult to mark visibly, without damage to their condition. You can use ultra-violet markers for such items. The marks should be renewed at least every two years and more often if the items are regularly cleaned or polished, or exposed to strong sunlight. Polyurethane varnish can be applied to ultra-violet markings, as it helps prevent fading.

Record of Valuables

Keep a list of all the valuables in the house or flat, including their financial worth, serial numbers, special characteristics, etc. Keep the list hidden.

Take photographs of items that cannot be marked, if possible using a Polaroid, so that potential thieves do not see the negatives. Place a ruler next to the valuables in each photograph, so that the size is obvious. Any negatives should be left with friends or relatives, at an address different from that of the items themselves.

Window Stickers

It is a good idea to put up window stickers announcing that items have been property marked. This deters burglars. Stickers can usually be bought with kits or separately from the same outlets that sell kits. Free stickers are also available from crime prevention officers and Neighbourhood Watches.

Specific Applications

1. Electrical Goods

Visible marking is best for TVs, radios, stereos, etc. Make the identifying marks with an engraver on the plastic or metal base, or else on the back of the item.

2. Cameras and Binoculars

Visible or invisible marking. Invisible marks are made on the inside of items, visible marks are made with an engraver on the outside.

3. Watches

Visible marks are made with an engraver on the back casing.

4. Gold, Silver, etc.

It is preferable to photograph these. They can be marked, visibly with an engraver, or invisibly, but great care is needed.

5. Jewellery

The problem is size. Many pieces are too small for marking. Photography is a good option. Police and jewellers will advise.

6. China or Porcelain

Invisible marks can be made on the base. Ceramic markers are also used. Photography is an option.

7. Glass

Apart from toughened glass, such as is used for car windows, glass is not really suited to visible marking with an engraver. The best method of visible marking is ceramic. Invisible marking is an option, along with photography.

8. Metal Clocks

Make visible marks on the base with an engraver. Photograph clocks of unusual design.

9. Wooden Clocks

These may be visibly marked with an engraver, although this can damage the wood. Make invisible marks inside the casing.

10. Clothing

Use a fabric marker or, for invisible marking, a spirit-based ultra-violet pen.

11. Handbags

Put the post code on the inside of the bag, using a ball-point pen. It is not a good idea to put the full name and address: the bag might carry keys allowing the burglar to get in.

12. Paintings

Make invisible marks on the back of the canvas. Paintings should always be photographed.

13. Bicycles

These are best marked, with specialist equipment, by police or a cycle shop.

ARTIFICE BURGLARY
by Bert Dady, Metropolitan Police

Artifice Burglary is the official title given to an offence which is becoming all too prevalent. It is better known to the public as 'The Conman at the Door'. The 'conman' can, however, be male or female, young or old. Most victims of this despicable crime are elderly and infirm. I refer to the crime as despicable because it takes advantage of the kindness and hospitality of victims and leaves them in fear and despair. It destroys their trust and makes the task of the genuine caller even harder.

But its greatest danger lies in the fact that where entry is gained, usually with a view to theft, much more serious crimes may then be committed.

How Do They Get In?

About 25% purport to have some connections with the water board. The rest put a lot of energy and sometimes skill into impersonating a range of people: social workers, electricity and gas board staff, collectors for charity, sales people, etc. Children and young people claim to be in search of lost balls; others claim to be women in distress, and carry babies.

What Do They Do When They Get In?

The usual method is for one or two callers to gain access to the victim's home and then one distracts the victim while the other searches and steals. Worst of all are occasions when the searching and stealing are done blatantly in front of the victim who is too elderly or infirm to intervene.

We must not forget the bogus builders and roof fixers who pressurize the elderly into having work done which may not even be necessary. They then charge exorbitant prices, after putting them in fear to get the money.

So What Can We Do?

Firstly, have a good quality chain fitted to the front door. *Use it all the time*. Put it on even before asking, 'Who is it?' Leave it on. You can talk to someone as long as you like providing you *keep your chain on*. However, always answer a call at the door – with the chain on, of course. Burglars will ring the bell to see if anyone is at home and will assume the house is empty if nobody answers.

There is no need to buy things at the front door. Most homes are within reach of shops and other facilities. Slight inconvenience and travel difficulties are preferable to what may happen if somebody untrustworthy gains access to your home.

The water board should not need to enter your house except in certain specific circumstances, such as water testing. Most of their work is done in the street. Be extremely wary of such callers.

Officials from the gas and electricity boards should know your account number. Get it from your bills. Print it in large letters and keep it pinned up behind the door where it can be seen only by you. If they cannot quote it do not let them in.

It is important to remember that the more persistent a caller is the more suspicious you should become. Genuine callers will respect your caution and will not mind returning another time (when someone else is with you).

Do not be afraid to investigate a caller. It is pointless spending a lot of money to secure your home if you then open your main door to anyone who cares to knock.

AFTER A BURGLARY

If you come home and suspect you have been burgled there are several things you must do immediately.

1. Be aware that the burglar may still be present. Ordinary citizens have the power of arrest and must decide for themselves

what they should do in such circumstances. Most burglars do not want confrontation with house occupants and are interested only in rapidly clearing the premises. A householder who similarly dislikes the prospect of such an encounter should give warning of their presence, by making as much noise as possible.

2. Go elsewhere, if you are unsure of what to do, and dial 999.

3. If at any point you see a burglar you should try to memorize their appearance. Make a note of it as soon as possible. Clothing is far easier to recall and identify than other physical attributes. So remember what they wore as well as skin and hair colour, age, height and build, etc.

4. Note the names and details of any police officers with whom you deal. This, during any investigation, makes liaison easier.

5. Householders, after a burglary, may return to an appalling mess in the most private parts of their home. Burglars, in their hurry, tend to tip everything out on to the floor (this is the easiest way to find hidden valuables). The understandable wish to tidy up, to get rid of the wreckage, must be resisted. Vital forensic evidence, especially fingerprints, will be damaged if touched.

6. Before police arrive you should try to assess what is missing and how the burglars entered.

7. Arrange for the repair of broken locks and fitments, within the constraints mentioned above, and with the advice of the local crime prevention officer.
8. Report lost credit cards and other missing papers and documents.

9. Tell your insurance company and request an insurance claim form.

10. Give a list of all identifiable items to the police and to the insurers.

11. In certain circumstances, or on request, police may contact the nearest victim support scheme. The support scheme will then make contact and offer help and advice.

INSURANCE

1. Reductions

Those who fit proper locks, chains and other security devices, or who belong to an active Neighbourhood Watch scheme, are often allowed considerable reductions on payments for house contents insurance.

2. Criminal damage

If you can, do take out additional insurance against criminal damage and attempted burglary. Quite often doors and windows are damaged during failed attempts at burglary.

3. Premiums

Obviously the amount you pay, in insurance premiums, rises if you are burgled. This is one more reason for ensuring you have good home security.

4. Records

Keep a careful record of house contents, room by room, object by object, estimating the value of each item. Update it regularly to ensure you are properly covered for all items you own. Tell the insurers immediately whenever you acquire new items. Insurance companies themselves will supply charts for list-making.

5. Small Print

Before taking out insurance read the small print of any agreements. If necessary, take all documents to a lawyer or insurance assessor. Advice on contract terms, and on all related matters, is available from the Association of British Insurers.

NEIGHBOURHOOD WATCH

What is Neighbourhood Watch?

Neighbourhood Watch is an association of individuals, in a particular locality, who band together to prevent crime, in co-operation with the police. The idea is that, by taking extra care and by being vigilant, crime will be prevented and controlled. Those involved hold regular meetings. They produce newsletters and leaflets and receive crime prevention advice from law enforcement agencies, which they then disseminate. Watches range in size from a few houses to hundreds of streets. There are many variations: Hospital Watch, School Watch, Cab Watch, etc. Yet the basic idea, which is that individuals should be active in their community to increase their own security from crime, remains constant.

The Development of Neighbourhood Watch

The idea was introduced to Britain from the USA in the early 1980s and grew rapidly in popularity. By the late 1980s it was claimed that there were about 100,000 active watches in England, Scotland and Wales, although the figure is extremely difficult to confirm. Taken up enthusiastically by the government, the watch concept has always been regarded with suspicion by the academic community and by other opinion-forming groups.

There was considerable opposition, at first, from certain Labour-controlled local authorities, who saw it as an attempt to bypass existing local infrastructures which they controlled. Senior police officers were at first extremely eager, but their subordinates often found the schemes difficult to resource and extremely time-consuming.

Does It Work?

The answer very much depends on whom you talk to. Academics and others in the criminology world tend to be critical, although it is hard to escape the feeling that some of this is coloured by ideological dislike of decentralized, populist, crime prevention schemes. Nobody says so directly, but the implication conveyed by the left-leaning criminological establishment is that watches are 'right-wing', attracting reactionary white middle-class suburbanites, and are therefore inherently suspect. There have been accusations of vigilantism and that schemes merely 'displace' crime from one area to another.

A crucial criticism is that watches have failed to stem the huge rises in property crime over the last few years. Supporters can always of course claim that the rises would have been even greater but for the effect of watch schemes, although this hypothetical contention is impossible to prove either way, for obvious reasons. Others maintain that lack of resources and support have prevented watches from fulfilling their potential. Academic studies have remained sceptical or ambiguous about schemes, but watch enthusiasts and some police officers continue to argue that properly resourced schemes can have a major effect on crime.

How It Works

Watches vary considerably in their mode of operation, although most of them will display most of the characteristics identified below.

1. Schemes are generally established when householders in a particular neighbourhood band together.

2. They hold a public meeting, supported by the police.

3. Co-ordinators, who take a supervisory role, are chosen.

4. A steering committee is appointed.

5. Newsletters and leaflets are printed, advising on crime prevention and local crime trends.

6. Householders who agree to participate put watch stickers in their windows, to deter criminals. They agree to look out for, and to report, suspicious behaviour in their locality.

7. Regular meetings are held.

8. Close liaison is maintained with crime prevention 'home beat' officers.

9. The co-operation of outside bodies, such as local authorities, local newspapers, and training agencies, is sought.

10. Sometimes watches take on a number of community and social functions, in addition to their main role. Indeed, improvements in neighbourliness and general community life are cited by supporters as examples of the benefits they bring.

Further Information

Those wishing to join or start a watch scheme should contact their local police who will advise. Crime Concern, the crime prevention organization, will also give advice and information (see Reference Section on p. 259).

5. Car Crime

INTRODUCTION

In the last few years those in authority, both in the police and in government, have given more and more attention to the question of car crime. Autocrime as a whole is no longer viewed as a slightly boring 'offence against property' which just happens to have an embarrassingly low clear-up rate. Autocrime has become a public and political issue.

This has one major cause: a massive and persistent increase in recorded offences of theft of and from cars. And, as noted, the rise in offences has not been accompanied by any significant rise in clear-ups.

In the decade from 1981 recorded car crime more than doubled, and normally composed above a quarter of all crime recorded in any given year. The problem intensified as the 1980s became the 1990s and the growth in this type of crime escalated.

To some extent this explosion may be caused by increased reporting of offences. But commentators emphasize that there are also far more cars for thieves to target than there were fifteen or twenty years ago, that the total grows constantly. Some observers see car crime rises as a symptom of the recession and the growth of an 'underclass', arguing that property crime ascends in tandem with rises in unemployment.

Another and crucial factor is that autocrime, at the moment, is relatively easy. Not only are there more cars to choose from, but a surprisingly large number of car owners take a fatalistic or careless attitude to the sort of basic security that hinders or deters thieves. What also favours the criminal is the decline of pedestrianism amongst police and public: if fewer people are on the street there are fewer potential witnesses or interveners to come between the casual thief and his goal.

Whatever its causes, autocrime absorbs vast police resources that could be better deployed elsewhere, and it is a major source of distress, expense and increased insurance premiums for the car-driving public. Government, police and other interested parties have come under great pressure to solve the resulting problems, especially as the news media have focused upon those killed or maimed by 'joyriders' in stolen cars. In the following pages we look closely at the whole issue.

The Public

The number of people directly affected by the threat of car crime has grown enormously over the past fifteen years. Between 1981 and 1987 alone, for example, the number of cars in Great Britain per 1000 people rose about 15%, from 281 in 1981 to 324 in 1987. This growth will continue, unless government policy and public attitudes change dramatically, which is unlikely, at least while the present government is in office. Autocrime therefore will become even more of an issue.

Those directly affected, who pay the higher insurance rates and bear the immediate inconvenience and cost, are not the only victims. The true costs of car crime affect everybody, driver and non-driver alike. The massive diversion of police resources and energy needed to fight, or even contain, escalating car crime means that there are fewer resources to devote to other, more pressing issues, such as street violence and mugging.

Although it has proved difficult for police and other authorities to persuade individuals to take preventive measures, this situation may slowly be changing. Media reporting has emphasized some of the more horrific consequences of joyriding, for instance; and autocrime has become associated in the public mind with generalized youth delinquency and social breakdown. Simultaneously government crime prevention campaigns have had an impact; the political opposition has also seen advantage in talking about the subject; and people are realizing exactly how much car crime costs them in increased insurance premiums. This will become even more pressing if insurance premiums are tied in more closely to crime prevention: those who have good security devices in their vehicles will pay less than others.

Yet the widespread impression remains that many members of the public still take a slapdash or careless attitude to the whole question. This fatalism seriously hinders the crime prevention endeavours of police and government. It is a little early yet to say whether recent campaigns, attempting to galvanize people about car security, will have a lasting impact on the public consciousness. For the moment casual attitudes to security mean that many people, including readers of this book, will get a nasty shock the next time they try to use their car.

The Criminals

Youthfulness. This is the characteristic most likely to be associated with those who steal cars or break into them. Many of them are younger than twenty, and the fourteen-year-old car thief is no great rarity. Proximity is another factor. Some car criminals are self-disciplined and dedicated, and select their targets carefully over a wide area, and penetrate them skilfully. But most of the young males who commit the bulk of autocrime dislike the effort needed in operating beyond places familiar to them. There is no requirement to travel far in any case. Plenty of soft, unprotected targets are within easy reach: their windows conveniently left open, their alarm systems faulty or non-existent . . .

If your car is broken into or stolen the likelihood is, then, that the thief is a very young man who lives not far from you. There is also a high chance that his mother has lived with several different partners during his childhood, and that he, like the rest of his family, has a poor employment and school record. Indeed, both he and his parents may never have had a 'proper' job. He has probably been sexually active since early puberty and is more promiscuous than average. He is a frequent user of recreational drugs and likes to drink. There is a good chance that his early experiments with drugs and drink began when he stole some from his mother and her then boyfriend. This was about the same time that he began breaking into cars and houses (burglary is his main interest apart from car crime). He is probably not very articulate, at least when with strangers.

None of this means that he cannot think. On the contrary, he probably has an extremely clear idea of how things operate in his life. He will know that there is little chance that he will be caught by the police. He will also be closely acquainted with the possibility that he will, if caught, get off with a formal caution. In any case, if prosecuted, he knows that he will, because of his youth, be assigned the sort of punishment that is unlikely to terrify him.

He will probably feel no guilt about his activities. In fact he may like to think of himself as a romantic outsider, a rebel whose background denies him the normal opportunities and who is thereby free of the normal social sanctions. Indeed, the media interest in what he does will, if anything, encourage his view of himself as a glamorous anti-hero. And recent governmental threats of 'sorting him out', of supplying him with 'a short sharp shock', do not worry him. He knows that talk doesn't stop criminals: and as far as he is concerned there is no sign that the talk is about to be exchanged for action. The next few years, with a major reshaping of the policing and justice system, will reveal whether his assessment continues to be correct.

The Police

One of the biggest embarrassments suffered by the police, over the last few years, has been their inability to do much about autocrime. The figures have risen and risen, with attendant publicity and growing public and governmental dissatisfaction.

The police have responded, especially during the Car Crime Prevention Year of 1992, with a range of prevention schemes and initiatives. Vehicle Watch is prominent amongst these (see below) and some of the projects set up are extremely imaginative and resourceful. It was difficult to assess, early in 1993, exactly how successful these projects had been, although there was some sign that the increases had begun to level off and even to recede a little, although a very major problem remains.

Yet many police officers feel that there is not much, in current circumstances, that they can do about the problem in the long term. Containment, or a slight reduction, is the best they can hope for unless, in the words of one officer, 'a few things are changed in the system'. The changes which police would most like to see, regarding car crime, are broadly the same as those they would like to see in other areas. They want to be involved much less in time-consuming administration and paperwork, and they are disillusioned with what they claim is the leniency of the sentencing system.

Cynicism about public attitudes is another element in the police view of the issue: 'People always complain. But they're not willing a lot of the time to take even the simplest precautions. Then when we turn up after somebody's reached through their unlocked car window they expect us to catch the villain in five minutes.'

There is also a strong feeling, amongst both senior and junior ranks, that car crime, like crime in general, is only partly a police problem. Society as a whole must sort its values out, with particular reference to youth culture, it is asserted, before crime can be controlled.

In the mean time police are under great pressure to do something, anything, about the problem. And they know that their reservations, about the extent of what they can achieve on their own, could backfire if they look like mere excuses for inefficiency. If that happened, whilst a massive review of the police is already underway, it could have serious consequences for the future of all aspects of the police service. The police, then, are trapped. They must continue to be energetic and purposeful about car crime, despite their own reservations about the ability of a purely policing response to make a major difference in this area.

The Government

Why did it take them so long? The political party which assumed
power in 1979 is very car-orientated, and has consistently pursued policies which encourage private transport, to the detri-
ment of buses and trains. The Conservatives, moreover, have
always presented themselves as being 'tough on crime'. Yet
despite steadily rising car crime, throughout the 1980s, it is
only recently that the subject seems to have caused any notable
brow-furrowing in the vicinity of the Cabinet.

This belated interest is probably because autocrime has
ascended even faster and higher in the last few years; and the
political opposition has seen electoral potential in crime issues
as a whole. The Labour Party, responding to the crime rates,
has now joined the Conservatives as a member of the talking-
tough club; Tony Blair, Labour's Home Affairs spokesman,
competes with the Conservatives in vigorously denouncing
criminal activity, although care is always taken to nod towards
the social concern which Labour has traditionally claimed to
exemplify. Speaking in February 1993, Mr Blair stated, 'There
are no excuses for crime and it is some of the poorest and most
vulnerable in our society that suffer its worst effects. This is
common sense. But so, equally, is the proposition that where a
community suffers poor education, bad housing, lack of employment . . . it is more likely to produce criminals than communities
where hope and opportunity exist for all.' The Liberal Demo-
crats also sustained the pressure on the government through
similar tactics. Further pressure is exerted on the government
by increased media coverage of general car crime, including
the joyriding which has severely afflicted parts of the country.
Another influential factor is widespread concern about youth
crime, which is of course closely linked to theft of and from
cars.

So far the principal governmental response, in England and
Wales, has been the 1992 Car Crime Prevention Year. A central
element in it was business and commercial sponsorship, in part-
nership with the Home Office and the police. This was in keeping with the government's philosophy of merging public and

private sector activity (see the section below on industry and commerce). A parallel campaign was mounted in Scotland. A dramatic 'hyena' logo was adopted for the campaign, depicting car criminals as scavenging animals. The campaign was officially launched in February 1992, with a multi-media advertising campaign and a variety of events and promotions to attract press and public interest. During the year over 5 million copies of a car security leaflet were distributed; 5600 'event days' were held by police forces in England and Wales; local authorities and crime prevention panels and similar groups also mounted local initiatives; 579 minutes of TV time were taken up by the campaign, plus 83 hours of radio and 10,000 column centimetres in the print media; the campaign was backed by 80 companies and trade associations.

Car security retailers and manufacturers reported increased sales, presumably as a result. Market research, the government claimed, indicated that two-thirds of people recognized the campaign's hyena symbol, 76% of motorists saw the campaign TV commercial, and two-thirds of those asked stated that the campaign made them more security-conscious.

At the end of 1992 the government claimed that recorded car crime in England and Wales, as a result of the above activities, had fallen 2½% in the three months between April and June '92, compared to the same period in 1991. For the government it will be important to see whether this modest improvement, after the massive rises of the last decade, is sustained.

How will government policy develop? In general terms the possibilities are exceptionally open. The administration which took office in 1992 has not been celebrated for the consistency of its viewpoint and the clarity of its planning. Furthermore, it is hard to specify what the implications, of the current review of policing and criminal justice, will be in this field. However, as mentioned before, subjects which the government is most likely to stress are quality control of car alarm and security systems, and the greater involvement of motorists in crime prevention.

Industry and Commerce

Two main types of industrial and commercial organization participate in the prevention of car crime. There are numerous specialist firms which make and sell everything from security devices to insurance services. And there are companies which have no direct connection with security or insurance. These, often in return for publicity or governmental approval, become involved in sponsorship and general support of crime prevention initiatives.

The government believes, or claims to believe, in the operation of the free market, and in the primacy of the private sector. However, a certain disorganization is an intrinsic problem of free markets. By definition those involved in them must compete and there cannot be central planning. This poses practical and ideological problems for governmental attempts to encourage the market in security devices and insurance to go in certain directions. If the government over-intervenes then the market is no longer free. If it does not intervene then the chaotic world of competing security firms and insurance companies will continue to offer a decidedly uneven and confusing service to the customer.

The problem is unavoidable. At present there is great variation in the quality of alarm systems, for instance. Some of them are very good. Some are very bad. There is an obvious case for regulation and quality control, but the government cannot be seen to order these things too directly. This would be to commit the unforgivable sin of 'interfering in the market'. Instead the government must encourage the market and its customers to 'choose' certain options. The best option in these circumstances is to tie car security as closely as possible to insurance. Thus the prospect of lower premiums is meant to entice car-owners into taking vigorous crime prevention measures. This is what is behind the government's support for the Motor Insurance Repair Research Centre (Thatcham) which we discuss later.

Persuading non-specialist companies to support crime prevention is less problematical, even during a recession. It is worthwhile, for such bodies, to co-operate with the desires of the

government and its agencies. And there is considerable publicity
to be gained from sponsoring good causes. There is no problem
with quality control, as the companies themselves are not
directly involved.

During the Car Crime Prevention Year about eighty private
sector organizations gave support. Competitions were spon-
sored, advertising campaigns were mounted, staff were given
appropriate training, literature was distributed. Those participating included Abbey National, the AA, the British School of
Motoring, Citroën UK, Cornhill Insurance, Dixons Group Ltd,
Gateway, General Accident, Honda, Sainsburys, Littlewoods,
Marks and Spencer, Mitsubishi, National Car Parks Ltd, the
RAC, Tesco.

The Media

Once car crime elicited a limited media response. This has
changed enormously as the sheer volume of such activity has
made it difficult to ignore. Crime prevention campaigns, like
Car Crime Prevention Year, have also drawn publicity, as has
the trauma suffered by those whose loved ones have been killed
or maimed by joyriders.

Yet coverage remains largely negative, especially in the major
media organizations. Often there is a strong implication that
car security measures are futile, that thieves will ultimately 'out-
wit' any security system.

This places the authorities in a double-bind. Media interest,
which they must cultivate in order to promote car security, also
increases performance pressure. For the publicity makes people
more aware of the government's failure to handle the problem,
and simultaneously much of it disparages the sort of preventive
measures which would help.

Research

There seems to be remarkably little university research into car crime. For instance, only a handful of some 200 research projects, listed in the 1992 Police Foundation Register of Policing Research, concerned this topic. Even historical criminology is slightly more popular as a research subject, on this evidence, than attempts to investigate autocrime. This is astonishing given the prevalence and cost of theft of and from cars, and the hundreds of millions of pounds distributed by the government, every year, for university research (not to mention the research money which universities get from private sector sources).

The omission signifies a poor return for taxpayers' money. This is particularly so as car crime and car security are ideal for the sort of interdisciplinary academic activity, involving both social scientists and technologists, that is now encouraged by the government and its agencies.

Outside the academic field, in the security and motor industry itself, and in general motoring organizations, there is evidence of a range of research activity, particularly into the effectiveness of car security systems. The Motor Insurance Repair Research Centre at Thatcham is important in this respect. Indications are that more such research will be undertaken, with strong governmental encouragement.

Case Study: Joyriding

'It's not like anything else. There's just nothing like it . . . Nothing to beat it. When you get hold of some wheels and do 130 down a motorway nobody can touch you.' Daniel, whose words these are, is fifteen years old and the experience he describes is called 'joyriding'. Joyriding, or stealing cars for the pleasure of driving them, is an increasingly popular and highly dangerous way of passing the time amongst teenage boys.

According to research figures 65% of stolen cars are taken

for 'temporary personal use' (joyriding). Many of those involved are under the age of seventeen. Often they began between the ages of thirteen and fifteen. The simple desire for thrills and 'daredevil' status is often the motive: 'I suppose it's as old as the hills. The need to show off,' one ex-joyrider remarked. The most popular vehicles are high-performance, with Ladas, Skodas and three-wheelers least likely to attract joyriding attention.

The risks are part of the attraction: 'The danger . . . you feel you're one up on it. One up on the odds when you do it . . .' Police estimate that many fatalities derive from joyriding. One study put the figure at about 1 in 9 of all fatal crashes. And the risks are not limited to the drivers. Passengers, pedestrians and police officers are also likely to suffer.

The issue has attracted national attention as the media have focused on the innocent victims. Steven Whittingham, twenty-seven years old, was one such victim. 'We think Steven had just popped out to put some petrol in the car,' his mother, Carol, was reported as saying. About 20 yards from his home, in Brighouse, Yorkshire, a car was doing 80 miles per hour downhill on the wrong side of the road. 'It hit Steven's car head on. He didn't have a chance. The car thieves' vehicle ended up in a playground where it burst into flames, trapping them inside.'

A friend of Steven's, who rushed up with a fire extinguisher, saved the lives of the joyriders. They ran off. It was too late to do anything for their victim. The eighteen-year-old driver, who had previous joyriding convictions, got three years' youth custody, 'which means he'll be out in a few months' time,' Steven's mother said, a year after the tragedy. The car's thirteen-year-old passenger, a 'habitual car-thief', was too young to face the courts. The Whittingham family are left with only their bitterness: 'They should call it "deathriding" not "joyriding,"' Carol Whittingham declares. And her experience of the criminal justice system has given her a very close view of just how twisted its operations can be: '*We* end up serving the life sentence.'

CAR SECURITY

New Technology

Technology is vital in car crime, by the very nature of motor vehicles. Car makers and security manufacturers are locked into a torrid and complicated relationship with thieves. The most professional and sophisticated of the latter are constantly seeking ways to bamboozle security devices fitted by the former. This conflict really only involves a minority, although a considerable one, of car thieves. Most ordinary car thieves do not have the sophistication, time or energy to study the methods used in penetrating advanced security systems. Nonetheless there is a trickle-down effect, as it were, from this high-level encounter between the latest security mechanisms and those trying to penetrate them. Eventually both the new security devices, and the attempts to foil them, work their way down into the lives of ordinary motorists and ordinary criminals.

Examples of devices which may move from the specialist arena into common usage are 'scanners' and 'grabbers'. Deployed at present mainly by the most professional thieves, these mechanisms scan and record the frequencies of electronic locking systems. Sometimes the criminals wait in cars until they spot a suitable vehicle. If the scanner does not immediately detect the security system's frequency a 'blocker' can be used, forcing the car owner to work the system again, so that the signal is grabbed at the second attempt. Of course cruder methods are available to the determined professional if technology fails. Cars can simply be lifted on to low-loaders and driven away. Motorbikes may be hidden in freezer vans that hide the noise of the alarm system.

An American example of the defences devised against such stratagems is Lojack, a mechanism that can be installed in as many as forty different places in a car. When a car equipped with this system is stolen microchips concealed in the vehicle enable police cars with tracking equipment to locate the car. A British version of this system, called Tracker, is now available from the AA.

Other manufacturers have produced locking methods that employ 'rolling codes'. The locking code changes each time the system operates. The aspirant thief picks up a code with his scanner that is already redundant when he replays it to get access. Even more advanced devices, derived from military coding techniques, are being prepared. These choose from billions of random codes whenever the system activates, making it almost impossible to break into the locking frequency.

Tagging devices, such as Yamaha's Datatag, have already been succesfully used. Five microprocessors are installed any- where on a motor-bike, allowing it to be traced even if dis- mantled. The makers claim that 5000 kits were sold between April 1992 and January 1993 and that only three tagged bikes were stolen.

Insurers, however, are not always optimistic about the impli- cations of using advanced security. Systems that immobilize the engine, after a break-in, can make a car less roadworthy for general purposes. Insurers also worry about standards. It is a fact that some systems just do not work as well as others. In response the Thatcham Motor Insurance Repair Research Centre is establishing itself, with government approval, as a validating agent. Car and car security makers are encouraged to send products to Thatcham for testing. Cars equipped with Thatcham-approved items will then, it is hoped, be eligible for lower insurance premiums.

At the moment some security firms themselves are putting most faith in advanced electronic tracking systems, which can follow a vehicle even if it is inside a trailer. Despite this there is every sign that the most sophisticated thieves will continue to engage, for the foreseeable future, in technological duels with the car security industry.

It must though be stressed that basic car security measures are always worth taking. Simple precautions, especially property marking, will slow down or deter even the most sophisticated criminals.

Case Study: Car Theft
By Glen Warren

It was hot. The massive parking area, car chrome ablaze in the sunlight, was almost full. The sprawling hypermarket it adjoined was crammed with families whose minds, amidst the air-conditioned shelving, were miles distant from the cars they had left a few yards away on the tarmac.

A clutch of kids entered the car-park, five of them. The eldest, a tall, skinny lad of about sixteen, had red hair and restless eyes. The others were a couple of years younger. All the boys wore the Floppy and Sloppy look that has charmed the nation's aesthetic sensibilities over the last few years: huge deconstructed T-shirts, shapeless trousers, back-to-front baseball caps. And they had the personal mannerisms that match such apparel: a smart-arse line in facial expressions, a sort of smug and untidy swagger. Anybody watching them might, though, have detected the fact that they were unusually quiet.

Halting, they looked round the mass of largely unattended cars. They conferred. Then the little band moved, again with surprising quietness, towards the far end of the car-park. They stopped, started again. The lanky leader, cropped hair catching tints of sunlight, surveyed the assembled vehicles, hand shielding his eyes. Then he halted. His gaze was caught by a little Japanese jeep, its glaring whiteness. Waving for the others to follow, he headed for it. Looking in, he liked its compact efficiency: it wasn't very big but the interior was constructed in a way that allowed maximum use of space. You could get a lot into it. He liked that. Liked things that were efficient. Walking round the car, he ran his fingertips over the body, wished the owners had dispensed with the pink stripe along the sides. Such things matter when you're sixteen, whatever your taste in clothing.

And it was at this point, as he stared at the jeep, as his mind slowly came to a decision, that two things nearly happened nearby. Both of them could have stopped him from pursuing a course that is only natural for badly dressed sixteen-year-old delinquents in slumbering car-parks. One of these near-events occurred inside the hypermarket. There the jeep's owner, for no particular reason, suddenly remembered that he hadn't activated the vehicle's alarm system. For a second he thought about going back out and rectifying things. And simultaneously, outside, the car-park attendant gave serious consideration to the possibility of leaving his little hut and taking a tour round his estate. But it was a hot day, and heat makes people lazy. The jeep-owner stayed dithering over the price of tomatoes and the attendant remained in his office. So neither event happened, and that left the way open for a third.

This did happen and it didn't take long. For the red-haired boy was quite practised. He leant close to the door and reached in his pocket, the other boys drawing close, their eyes suddenly alert, scanning the whole area around. Their leader looked up once, met their eyes, nodded, and then, with something he took from his pocket, he performed an obscure and decisive act against the car door. He pushed once, and the door was open. The youth froze for a second, waiting for the alarm, ready to bolt, but nothing happened. He grinned. The others rushed him. They all piled in, giggling and jostling.

The stocky little vehicle swept from the car-park, windows down, sun roof open. An elbow rested on the window frame, music blasting from the speakers. The attendant, slumbering over his paper, raised his head when he heard the noise, but only briefly. He was used to noisy car stereos. Inside the hypermarket the car owner was happily piling his trolley with goods. When you've got well-designed transport it doesn't matter how much shopping you get in one go, he reflected. The jeep will carry it all, with room to spare. Outside, the jeep moved into the distance, its music audible long after it disappeared.

Prevention of Car Crime

As with burglary the main threat to cars derives from the activities of the casual, opportunist thief, although specialist operators pose more of a threat than in burglary, particularly as far as expensive or very new cars are concerned. It is worth remem-

bering, nonetheless, that although the minority of skilled operators may be able to penetrate many car security systems, they
will still lose time in the process and are thereby more likely to
be seen and caught.

When police use the term 'autocrime' they mean both theft
of cars and theft from cars.

1. *Theft of Cars*. This category encompasses cars stolen for
joyriding and others which are carefully selected so that they
may be resold in disguised or altered form. Some thieves
specialize in the practice of equipping a stolen car with false
papers and other marks of identity. Sometimes the car is partially
or wholly dismantled and the parts sold.

Many stolen cars, whose drivers can be as young as twelve,
are involved in 'joyriding' accidents, causing death and serious
injury. In some areas 'ram-raiding' is hugely popular: young
men steal cars and use them as battering rams to break into
shops and houses, before escaping in the same vehicles.

2. *Theft from Cars*. There is a thriving criminal trade in car
radios and music systems and other items removed from parked
cars. In some places, also, theft occurs while cars are at traffic
lights.

3. *Personal Safety*. Great concern has been expressed, in the last
few years, about the threat to people whose cars are stopped by
strangers, or who are alone in isolated places when their cars
break down. The risk of such attack is actually very low. Nonetheless motorists should see the relevant entry in the section on
self-protection, and also the entry, in this section, on motoring
organizations.

4. *Garages*. Cars are much safer when garaged. If you have a
garage put the car in it, and lock both it and the car.

5. *Vehicle Watch*. Car watch schemes are rapidly becoming
popular. They are especially suited to those who drive for only
part of the day. See the relevant entry in this section of the book.

6. *Buying a Car.* When purchasing any sort of car, whether new or second-hand, ask about security mechanisms. See the information given below.

7. *Selling a Car.* Fraud is growing as a part of car crime. Be very careful, when selling a vehicle or its parts, about accepting cheques. The use of false building society cheques is becoming more popular in this respect.

8. *Identification.* Do not leave anything in a car which gives your home address. Do not leave vehicle documents, such as registration papers, MOT or insurance certificates, in the car. They could be of great help to a thief in selling your car, or in providing a false identity for another stolen vehicle. It is especially important that you do not leave credit cards in your car. Much credit fraud is based on cards stolen from vehicles.

9. *Strangers.* Watch out for those on the street who show interest in your car. Some of them may be planning to steal it or its contents or parts. Note their appearance and dress.

10. *Motoring Organizations.* Several of the leading car-user organizations, such as the AA and the RAC, give safety and crime prevention advice.

Prevention of car crime falls into two main areas of discussion: 'target hardening' and protective devices. Target hardening is about all the general ways in which the thief's job can be made difficult or impossible; protective devices are mechanisms and fitments which stop and/or deter a criminal from driving a car or from threatening its contents.

Theft from Cars: Target Hardening

1. Parking

A garage is the safest parking place. If this is not feasible then the car should be in a well-lit location which is not isolated and which is near houses or offices.

The best public car-parks are those which are supervised, and which have controlled exits and entrances, security cameras and adequate lighting. Do not use badly lit car-parks, or those which are empty or have vegetation that camouflages criminal activity. In a car-park the safer spots are nearer to the entrance and well lit. In an open car-park the best place is in the middle, not round the edge where foliage and walls may be used as cover by criminals.

Be careful with parking tickets, especially those which are displayed on the windscreen and reveal how long the car is likely to be parked.

See the section below on secured car-parks.

2. Valuables

a. Do not leave valuables in cars. They tempt thieves. Even the sight of a bulging shopping bag is enough to suggest to the passing criminal that other goodies may also be available. If leaving things in the car is unavoidable then remember to conceal them. Use a blanket or a sheet, or conceal items under seats or in the boot or the glove compartment. Do not leave newly purchased goods, such as television sets or stereos, in parked cars, even for a while. Leave them at the shop until they can be collected.

b. Car radios and cassettes, phones, portable stereos and other electronic hardware should be removable, and where possible should be taken from the car when parked. The small size of such items, which means that they are easy for thieves to carry, also means that they are easy for car owners to take with them. A shoulder bag can be kept in the car for this purpose, but obviously should never be left in the car, as this would help a thief in transporting stolen goods.

c. Ensure that all basic car locks work properly and are in good overall shape. Check what sort of locks there are for the sun roof, side windows, bonnet, boot, and glove compartment. Replace locks that are wearing out. Check quarterlight windows to ensure they shut. In older vehicles they are often a means of entry. Best of all are deadlocking systems. With these, even if a window is broken, the door cannot be opened by reaching in and operating the door lock button.

d. Check all locks every time you leave the car.

3. Alarms and Immobilizers

Install a car alarm that will respond to all attempts to break in. Regularly check that all alarm systems are working. Install an electronic immobilizer that will disable the fuel, starter or ignition of the vehicle, to defend against 'hotwiring'. Mechanical immobilizers are able to lock the steering wheel or gears.

4. Property Marking

Car fitments, especially radios and cassettes, must be property-marked. See the property-marking section under Home Security. Security stickers, warning thieves of this, should be prominently displayed.

5. Aerials

Aerials should be retractable. Retract them every time the car is parked in the open. The best types are self-retracting and controlled by the ignition.

6. Moving Cars

In some areas thieves have been known to reach in, or break glass, to get at handbags and valuables while cars are waiting at traffic lights or in jams. Keep doors and windows locked at such points and keep thievable objects out of sight as much as possible. Do not stop the car for anybody who acts suspiciously, especially in lonely places.

7. Service Stations

Do not leave valuables in cars, even for just a few minutes, when using service station facilities. Always lock the car, however briefly you are outside it, even when filling the tank with petrol.

Theft of Cars: Target Hardening

1. Age and Design

Cars older than ten or fifteen years are easier to penetrate. They are less conspicuous and harder to protect. They are, therefore, much easier to steal than newer vehicles. At the other extreme, the very newest and smartest cars are targeted by professional thieves who remove identification from the vehicle and resell it abroad. Owners of such vehicles should use the most advanced and reliable car security mechanisms.

2. Locking

Ensure that no car is left unattended, however briefly, without locking the doors, windows and boot. Anti-theft fitments should also be activated and given regular maintenance.

3. Alarms and Immobilizers

Ensure that all alarms and immobilizers are functioning and that they are properly maintained.

4. Ignition Key

Never leave the ignition key in the car, even if it is in your own garage.

5. Service Stations

See the entry under Theft from Cars.

6. Stickers

Put deterrent stickers in your car window, telling thieves that the vehicle has security devices. Do this even if security mechanisms are not fitted: it will still deter.

7. Parking

See the entry under Theft from Cars. Note the comments on parking tickets, and the fact that the absence of a ticket makes it harder for a thief to take a car from a car-park which has a check-out system. Therefore if the car-park is not pay and display you should keep the ticket with you when you leave the vehicle.

Wherever you park you should choose a place that is well lit. If you park in the street keep the front wheels turned sharply towards the kerb. This makes it harder to tow the car away.

8. Property Marking

The car's registration number should be visibly marked on all its windows. The best place is at the top of each window, so that the marks cannot be hidden by just winding the windows down a small distance. Such marking makes it hard for thieves to give the car new number plates and documents for resale. Criminals must then go through the expense and awkwardness of replacing the glass, with the accompanying risk of arousing suspicion.

Protective Devices

There are many alarms, immobilizers and locking systems that prevent autocrime. The technology changes rapidly, but the following are examples of the basic systems and security strategies which are most widely used.

1. Car Radios, Cassettes, Telephones

These items are very popular with opportunist thieves and should be as portable as possible, so that you may remove them when the car is left. Otherwise they can be locked in the boot. If such options are not available then disguise is possible. With some radio cassettes, for example, plastic covers are available which fold down when the system is inoperative. Other radio cassettes are security-coded. The code is keyed in when the radio is installed. After it is taken from the car the radio cassette will not work unless the correct code is used. Some variants lock into position automatically when the driver's door is locked or when the ignition is switched off. Warning stickers deter and stop thieves from damaging the car in futile attempts to steal.

2. Wheels

Thieves also steal wheels which they resell on the black market. Lockable wheel nuts, sold in packs of four, offer a good protection.

Wheel clamps, such as those used by traffic wardens, are available commercially, and will completely immobilize a wheel. However they are cumbersome and expensive, and their usage, even on all four wheels, will not prevent the car being removed on a trailer. Really desperate thieves can cut through the clamps with welding or drilling equipment, although this is obviously noisy and attention-attracting.

3. Petrol

Petrol is easily siphoned from the fuel tank. Vandals may put things in the tank which damage the engine. Fit a lockable fuel cap and an anti-siphoning device.

4. Roof Racks and Trailers

Remote sensor alarms are available for installation on roof racks and trailers.

5. Handbrake Combination Lock

A three digit combination lock can be fixed to the handbrake. This will, of course, make the car extremely hard to drive. This is an example drawn from the huge range of mechanical immobilizers.

6. Handbrake and Gear Stick

A lock is available that is attached to both the gear stick and the handbrake. A thief cannot, therefore, take the handbrake off or put the car into gear. This also is just one of many different kinds of mechanical immobilizers.

7. Electronic Engine Lock

This stops the engine from starting until the right code is keyed into a touchpad attached to the dashboard.

8. Ultrasonic Alarms

These give off ultra sound waves. A thief trying to get into the car upsets the frequency pattern of the waves and so the alarm starts.

9. Infra-Red Alarms and Locking Systems

An infra-red transmitter is put on the driver's key tab. This is aimed towards the receiver in the car, and when a button on the tab is pressed the doors lock and the alarm is set. Unlocking and switching off are controlled by the same method. Similar systems can be operated by radio frequency.

10. Trembler Switch Alarms

A ball bearing is set between a pair of contacts. Any significant motion of the car makes the ball bearing touch the contacts and sets off the alarm.

11. Passive Alarms

This type of alarm is ready to function once the car is locked. It gives the owner time to enter the vehicle before it sounds and is controlled by a hidden switch inside the car. Once operational it is triggered by all but the slightest movements.

12. Ignition Cut-Out Systems

These systems are examples of classic immobilizers. They block the ignition and fuel and starter, and are often linked to the car horn so that it simultaneously sounds the alarm.

13. Voltage Drop Systems

Controlled by a key or a switch. The alarm sounds when a sensor in the car's electrical circuit detects voltage falls, such as those which occur when courtesy lights come on or because the door opens.

14. Pin-Switch Alarms

The mechanism is wired to the car door. If the door opens the pin emerges from the switch, earthing the electrics and starting the alarm. Other parts of the vehicle may also be fitted with this system.

15. Pendulum Alarms

A small weight is fixed to a spring. Beneath the weight is an electrical contact. When the car is knocked, bumped, or pushed the spring moves. The weight moves in response, touching the contact. The alarm then sounds. The problem with this system is its hyper-sensitivity. Passing vehicles can trigger it needlessly, as can pavement activity. Adjustments, to counter this, are possible, but it often remains a problem.

16. Lights

Flashing lights, to reinforce the sound effects, can be added to most alarm systems.

17. DIY Systems

Do-it-yourself kits, allowing car owners to put their own security mechanisms together, are quite widely available. Care, as always, should be exercised with installation and maintenance.

Take the advice of a crime prevention officer before exploring
this option.

Case Study: the Care-Lesses

Anthony and Jessica Care-Lesse have just moved into an untidy
semi-detached house in North London. Anthony is an architect
in his late thirties. He wears dark suits for work and denim and
corduroy at the weekend. Jessica, who qualified as a solicitor,
is a few years younger and is small and vivacious, in contrast
to her large and laconic spouse. She left work to bring up their
two children, Sam and Joe, now aged 2 and 3 years respectively.
The boys' sturdy, dungaree-wearing names reveal something
about how the Care-Lesses want the world to view their little
family. 'I think basically we're rather pragmatic, although open
minded sort of people . . . not the types to get too het up about
anything . . .', says Anthony. Anthony says 'basically' and 'sort
of' rather a lot in a manner that hints at deliberate self-parody
(you get the feeling that he likes to think of himself as being
'ironic').

Jessica, sitting in the garden in her floral smock and leggings,
agrees with her husband about their approach. 'I think we're
fairly easy-going. You can't ruin your life worrying about what
might happen. We try to balance things'. As she says this her
husband's eyes glint across at her through his sunglasses. 'That's
the word, ' he emphasizes. 'Balance.' He pauses, frowning, as
if worrying that somebody might accuse him of being literal,
direct. Then he smiles, as if he has worked it all out, and adds
a couple of his famous qualifying phrases: 'I think. Sort of.'
They both laugh. That's all right then. Anthony is being *so*
ironic.

And that is what they are like, the Care-Lesses. They want
things to work both ways, so that they can be serious about
such matters as 'balance', and frivolous at the same time. Long-
ago they acquired the idea that this sort of ambiguity is sophisticated, worldly. But their concept of balance is far cruder than

they could imagine, and is about to get them into trouble. Because what it means, in terms of security, is that they put a very limited effort into protecting their possessions.

The Care-Lesses are fatalistic about property crime. 'Theft is the price you more or less pay for living in London', is how Anthony puts it. It's as if they feel, subconsciously, that life has been so easy that they must, somehow, propitiate the gods of Balance by making things hard for themselves in other ways.

And so it is that neither of their cars has a proper locking system. Jessica has an alarm on her BMW that doesn't work and a steering wheel lock that she frequently forgets to fit. Anthony often doesn't even bother to shut all his windows.

And making things hard for themselves is exactly what they are doing, although they do not yet know it. It is only a matter of time before the local car thieves, operating from the large estate down the road, spot the potential of Anthony's sports car, of Jessica's BMW. And when they come for the cars they will also note the interesting and relatively unsecured nature of the Care-Lesse dwelling in general.

Not that the full potential of this fact will be exploited by the local villains immediately. There is no hurry. There are plenty of other families nearby who take an easy-going approach to these matters. When they finally get into the house, of course, they will make a thorough job of it in a manner that might traumatize the owners beyond all their experience.

But none of this is evident to the Care-Lesses as the birds twitter around them in their garden. The idea that their lax attitude to car security may have all these complicated reverberations is unknown to them. Life is quite pleasant provided you know what you are about. 'It's all down to the B-word', Anthony declares, with deliberate exaggeration They both laugh. Anthony is pleased with himself. He's found a new way of being ironic.

Asking For It?

Is the massive rise in car crime at least partly the fault of careless owners? Research, both by the Home Office and by the AA, suggests that this may be so. The AA, in fact, says that up to a million motorists a day leave their car keys in the ignition while they go off to pay for their petrol. After questioning 300 motorists over three days, at a petrol station on the London-Eastbourne road, the AA discovered that 24% of them admitted they 'always' or 'sometimes' left the ignition keys in their cars for an average of at least three minutes when paying for their petrol. Men were considerably more careless than women. Obviously this is a small sample in a small area, but if nationally consistent it suggests that a million people a day, on garage forecourts, leave their vehicles wide open to casual theft. The problem, the AA stresses, could become even worse as more people pay by time-consuming credit card (the AA figures are given in more detail below).

An earlier AA survey found that 10% of cars in a town centre car-park were unlocked. Home Office research estimates that 12% of drivers leave their cars unlocked at least occasionally. Whatever the exact figures may be, and survey investigation is particularly prone to distortion because of methodological problems, such research reinforces what police officers have claimed for years, on the basis of their own experience: 'When it comes to autocrime some people are just asking for it.'

The AA Petrol Station Survey
(Reproduced from the *AA Magazine*, Autumn 1992)

Three hundred drivers were asked: 'When going to pay for your petrol, do you leave your car keys in the ignition?' Replies were as follows: Always: 22 (7.3%). Sometimes: 50 (16.7%). Never: 228 (76%). Of those who replied Never, 30% said it was because the petrol cap key was on the same key-ring as the ignition key.

Analysis of the figures shows that 85 women were interviewed and that they replied as follows: Always: 1 (1.2%). Sometimes: 14 (16.5%). Never: 70 (82.4%).

Of the 215 men interviewed, the response was: Always: 21 (9.8%). Sometimes: 36 (16.7%). Never: 158 (73.5%).

Of the 22 who said they always left their keys in the ignition, two said their cars were not worth stealing, one thought forecourts were very safe places, one woman left her very small daughter in the car and and one man said his key was stuck, so he had no option. One man left a brand-new BMW complete with keys and another a brand-new Mercedes Benz.

Buying a Car

Buying a New Car

Many choices face someone buying a new car: cost, reliability, roadworthiness, etc. Far too few people include security in this list of vital considerations. Yet it is pointless spending money on a new machine only to lose the use of it before you have time to enjoy the benefits it brings.

Searching questions must be asked. What sort of security devices are already fitted to the vehicle? Are they easy to operate? How difficult is it to fit alternative or extra security mechanisms? All these things affect not only the crime risks attached to the car, but also the insurance you pay. You will pay higher premiums if you have been a car theft victim, and the government is generally encouraging insurance companies to offer lower premiums to those whose cars have good security fitments.

Specific items that should be part of any new car you buy are as follows:

1. Security-marked windows, internal equipment and panel.

2. Immobilizing mechanism (which stops a car starting when a thief gets in).

3. A standard car alarm.

4. Deadlocks fitted to the doors.

5. A central locking system.

6. A lockable fuel cap.

7. Lockable wheel nuts.

8. A security-coded or detachable car radio and cassette player.

Buying a Used Car

Large numbers of cars are purchased second-hand. Most trans-actions are uncomplicated, but there is always a risk of buying a stolen vehicle. Much trouble is caused when this happens and the buyer often loses both money and peace of mind. If a car acquired from a reputable dealer turns out to be stolen then a full refund should be available, particularly if the seller belongs to the Retail Motor Industry Federation, or the Scottish Motor Trade Association.

Basic precautions, as outlined below, reduce the risk:

1. Advertisements detailing times to telephone should be treated warily; occasionally the numbers given are those of a call box or of a third party.

2. Go to see the vehicle at the seller's premises; do not have it brought to you. This gives you the chance to assess the seller: is he an honest individual trying to get rid of an unwanted asset, or could he be a dealer of a less than reputable kind?

3. When you view the car look for signs confirming that the seller actually lives at the address.   .

4. Watch for evidence of casual car-dealing: spare parts scattered around, other cars nearby which are obviously under repair. (This is not of course to suggest that all or even most casual car-dealing is outside the law, but it is a fact that the malpractice that does exist flourishes more in an informal environment.)

5. Ensure that chassis and engine numbers are identical to those on the documents.

6. Examine the registration papers. Note how long the vehicle

has been owned by the seller; be careful if this has only been for a short while. If there is no registration document ask the seller how long he has owned the car; be suspicious if he says he has had it a long time but has no documents.

7. Other things to scrutinize in the registration paper are water-marks, typeface, over-typing, spelling errors. Anything that does not fit may betray a forgery.

8. Remember that photocopies have no legal validity.

9. Be suspicious of mechanical features that do not match (these may indicate that the car combines parts from several, stolen vehicles). An example would be high-performance trimmings and badges on a low-performance car.

10. Anyone buying at auction should take up low-cost indemnity clauses. These give protection if the vehicle turns out to be stolen, saving time, expense and trouble.

After Purchase

Replace any security mechanisms, especially door locks, that are not in good condition. If they are not already fitted, add security marking and devices such as lockable fuel caps.

Thatcham: The Motor Insurance Repair Research Centre

This organization has been given the task, by major insurance companies, of assessing car security standards. Based at Thatcham in Berkshire, it launched a new project, the Insurance Industry Vehicle Security Scheme, in January 1993. 'The aim of the Scheme is to evaluate security systems...' the Centre declares, 'against set criteria and to inform insurers and other interested bodies of those security systems that meet the criteria.'

Companies and individuals voluntarily submit devices for

testing, for a fee. Those mechanisms passing the tests will get the Centre's approval. The insurance companies will then be notified that the particular car security system has satisfied 'the requirements of the British Insurance Industry Criteria for Vehicle Security'.

The aim is to encourage insurance companies to link premiums to the quality of security systems fitted to particular cars. Lower premiums would be available to cars with good security.

This project, which has strong governmental approval, is very important. Its voluntary basis fits in with the government's free-market ideology, and if it is successful it will be seen as a pacemaker for other initiatives of a similar kind.

Secured Car-Parks

Target-rich adventure playgrounds, crammed with opportunities. That is how thieves often perceive public car-parks: 'It's a gem,' said one criminal, talking about a car-park in a provincial city. 'Custom-built for stealing, that place. It's got everything you want, just laid on: it's badly lit, the attendants are in a daze, there are no proper cameras, no notices telling people to be careful, there's lots of little corners and stairwells, a lot of bushes and trees round the edge . . . it's a gem.'

The Home Office, recognizing the existence of such gems, launched a Secured Car-Parks scheme in September 1992. The project, initiated by the Association of Chief Police Officers and administered by the AA, aims to improve security in existing public and private car-parks and to encourage the 'designing-in' of security features during the planning of new sites.

Car-park owners and operators wishing to be considered for the scheme apply to their local police. Premises are then inspected according to detailed specifications about such topics as lighting, visibility, supervision, etc. Car-parks reaching the required security level receive awards, of either gold or silver, depending on the level attained.

Notices about the award are displayed and obviously attract

customers, giving the parks concerned an obvious advantage and an incentive to maintain security. Regular inspection, by those controlling certification, ensures standards are upheld.

By November 1992 twenty car-parks had already received awards. These are listed below.

Barnsley, Alhambra Shopping Centre
Basildon, Savacentre Car-Park. East Gate Shopping Centre
Canterbury, St John's Nursery Car-Park
Canterbury, Sturry Road Park and Ride
Cardiff, Capitol Exchange Car-Park
Cardiff, Tredegar Street NCP
Cardiff, Cardiff International Hotel Car-Park
Heathrow, Apcoa Business Park
Heathrow, Scylla Road Park and Fly
Heathrow, Flightpath Long-Term Car-Park
Huddersfield, Queensgate Multi-Storey Car-park
Llandudno, Victoria Centre Car-Park
Luton, Airport Car-Park 'C'
Manchester, Airport Long-Stay Car-Park '3'
Newcastle, Eldon Garden Multi-Storey
Nottingham, Trinity Square Car-Park
Stafford, Guildhall Shopping Centre Park
Watford, King's Car-Park
Watford, Queen's Car-Park
Winchester, Brooks Centre Car-Park

MOTOR-CYCLE SECURITY

Motor-bike theft is a major phenomenon. The Home Office estimates that, between 1987 and 1992, 115,000 bikes valued at around £70 million were stolen and were never recovered. Yet it was estimated that by 1992 fewer than half the UK's 900,000 bikes had security fitments. Insurance premiums, in consequence, have virtually doubled in the recent period.

Both opportunist and professional thieves see motor-cycle

theft as a fairly uncomplicated activity. Unsecured bikes can be put into vans without great effort or are simply wheeled away. The professional will target a specific type, for carefully planned resale, or to be used as parts for other vehicles. The casual criminal will be after quick cash or a bout of joyriding.

Precautions Against Theft

Although motor cycles are obviously easier to steal than cars it is still worthwhile securing them. Good security devices can deter and/or prevent both casual and dedicated thieves.

Parking

1. Vary your parking place.
2. If possible use a car-park with a 'Secured Car-Park' sign. This means it has been verified as having a high standard of security.
3. In daylight park in a busy public place.
4. Park in properly lit places after dark.
5. Look for specially built motor-bike parking areas, especially those with fixed parking stands or bays.

Locking

1. Never leave valuables, such as a crash helmet, in pannier bags or otherwise attached to the bike.
2. The steering lock should always be activated.
3. Preferably use high tensile steel cable and a good padlock to tie the bike to a fixed object or another bike. A U-lock, through the rear wheel or bike frame, may also be used.

Alarms

Motor-cycle alarms are sold at DIY or bike shops. Make sure the alarm is evident to a prospective thief. A warning sticker on the bike helps to deter.

Marking

The bike is easier to trace, harder for a thief to sell, and easier to reclaim if stolen, if it is marked with a post code or registration number or Vehicle Identification Number (VIN). See the entries on property marking under Home Security for details of how this is done.

Validation

Ensure that you buy security equipment which is of a good standard. Advice on what and where to buy is supplied by the Motor-cycle Retailers' Association.

Watch Schemes

Motor-cycle crime prevention schemes are an effective means of enhancing security. Motor-cycle organizations, as well as local police officers, provide information about where and when these groups meet. Below we list two such bodies.

1. The Motor-cycle Action Group

This is a national network of 120 groups, based around the country. It aims to further the rights of motor cyclists and to upgrade motor-bike security. Members are eager to assist those wishing to join or set up local organizations.

2. The Norfolk Motor-cycle Dealers' Crime Prevention Association

The association comprises more than forty motor-cycle dealers. They are interested in bike security issues as a whole, but also have a 'hotline' linking them to the Norfolk police, enabling them to report any suspect machines brought to them for repair or service.

Registration

Do not let criminals get hold of registration papers. They can be used by thieves in selling your own bike or in disguising some other stolen bike. If, at any point, a motor bike becomes an insurance 'write-off', then the insurer should pass the registration papers to the DVLA.

Buying Motor Cycles

New Motor Cycles

When buying a new bike consider the following points:

1. How many security devices are built into the machine?

2. Are there identification numbers, an immobilizer, and a fitted alarm?

3. If any of these are missing will the dealer fit them for a fair price?

Second-Hand Motor Cycles

Remember the following when buying a second-hand bike:

1. A photocopy of a registration document is legally worthless.

2. Ensure that you see the original registration document.

3. Check whether the name on the registration is that of the seller or of someone else.

4. Is there evidence that the bike's frame or engine number has been changed?

5. Is the frame or engine number identical to that on the registration papers?

6. Is there proof of the seller's name and address?

7. Be careful if the seller is particularly eager to meet away from their home (this might be because they do not want to be traced or identified).

Motor-Cycle Dealers

Those who sell bikes should always check the credentials of any machines brought in for service, especially if duplicate keys are requested.

VEHICLE WATCH

A concept rapidly becoming popular, in the struggle against autocrime, is Vehicle Watch. Based on North American initiatives, this entails attaching stickers to vehicle windscreens, signifying that the owners want their vehicles stopped by police if they are seen being driven between certain hours. Often the hours are late at night. This is important, for much car crime occurs during darkness. In most schemes the curfew period, when the car can be stopped, is between midnight and 5 a.m. Luckily police are not so busy at this time and resources are easier to allocate than at other periods.

Scheme membership also brings other benefits. Participants can be introduced to a variety of car security techniques, for example security marking, central locking systems.

But how effective and popular is Vehicle Watch? Sergeant Jonathan Brown, of Gwent Constabulary, conducted research into the topic. He discovered that many forces already operate schemes. In Gwent Constabulary's first 9 months of operating the scheme he found that about 19% of all the county's vehicle owners joined. 'Analysis of crime data to date suggests that crime rates for members (in Gwent) are lower than those for non-members,' a Home Office summary paper commented. Also noticeable was an improved attitude towards the police and the quality of service they offer.

Of course, the whole matter is still at an early stage. Vehicle Watch is open to all the ambiguities that have dogged its domestic model, Neighbourhood Watch, and there is a whole range of methodological ammunition available to those who instinctively distrust this sort of approach to crime prevention. 'It is also difficult to assess to what extent the improvements identified in Gwent are attributable to Vehicle Watch and to what extent they are attributable to other factors,' the Home Office said. It is always possible that those joining schemes, for instance, are those more likely to take precautions anyway, and that these people would be less at risk in any circumstances. Or the fall in crime may have occurred because criminals in the watch area have displaced to other less 'target-hardened' localities.

The main practical difficulty is the need for drivers to abide by a self-imposed curfew. And police, as with Neighbourhood Watch, may find schemes hard to resource if they become really popular. Despite these qualifications, and they are typical of the doubts that attend virtually all crime prevention initiatives, Vehicle Watch definitely seems worthy of further exploration.

THEFT RISK FOR DIFFERENT VEHICLES

How likely is it that your car will be stolen?

The table below is based on a Home Office assessment of the theft risk for different vehicles in England and Wales. The Home Office explains that 'the risk of theft has been calculated by taking the numbers of each range stolen during a period and dividing this by the average number of cars within each range on the road during the period.' The final calculations are based on 'an average theft rate for each range'. It is stressed that 'this may disguise much higher or lower theft rates for parts of the range . . . higher performance cars within each range are much more likely to be stolen whilst estate versions of each range are less likely to be stolen.'

The cars are classified as high, medium, and low risk, and are in alphabetical order within each category.

High Risk

Ford Capri Mk2; Ford Capri Mk3; Ford Cortina Mk2; Ford Cortina Mk3; Ford Cortina Mk4; Ford Cortina Mk5; Ford Escort Mk1; Ford Escort Mk2; Ford Fiesta Mk1; Ford Granada Mk2/3; Rover Metro Mk2; Vauxhall Astra Belmont; Vauxhall Astra Mk2.

Medium Risk

Alfa Romeo 75; Alfa Romeo Alfasud; Alfa Romeo Alfetta; Alfa Romeo Giulietta; Audi 90; Audi Coupe; Aus/Mor 1100/1300; Aus/Mor 1800; BMW 1/2/3000 series; BMW 300 series; BMW 500 series (E12); BMW 500 series (E28); BMW 600 series (E24); BMW 700 series (E23); Dacia (all ranges); Daihatsu Fourtrak Mk1; Daihatsu Fourtrak Mk2; Daimler Sovereign.

Fiat 132; Fiat Croma; Fiat Mirafiori; Fiat Strada Mk1/2; Ford Capri Mk1; Ford Classic/Corsair; Ford Escort Mk3; Ford Fiesta Mk2; Ford Fiesta Mk3; Ford Granada Mk1; Ford Granada Mk4; Ford Orion Mk1; Ford Sierra Mk1; Ford Sierra Mk2; Ford Sierra Sapphire; Hillman Minx; Honda Integra; Isuzu Trooper.

Jaguar XJ/XJS; Lada 1300; Lancia Beta; Lancia Delta; Lancia Thema; Landrover Discovery; Lotus Eclat; Mazda 323 Mk3; Mazda Montrose; Mazda RX; Mitsubishi/Colt Celeste; Mitsubishi/Colt Cordia; Mitsubishi/Colt Lancer; Mitsubishi/Colt Sapporo; Mitsubishi/Colt Shogun; Mitsubishi/Colt Sigma; Morris Minor.

Nissan/Datsun Bluebird Mk1; Nissan/Datsun Patrol; Nissan Datsun Silvia; Nissan/Datsun Silvia; Nissan/Datsun Violet; Nissan/Datsun Z/ZX; Opel Ascona; Opel Kadett; Opel Manta; Opel Senator; Peugeot 504; Peugeot 604; Porsche 911; Porsche 924; Porsche 928; Porsche 944.

Range Rover; Renault 30; Rover 2000; Rover 3000; Rover 200 Mk2; Rover 400; Rover Maestro; Rover Metro; Rover Mini; Rover Montego; Saab 900; Seat Marbella; Simca 1100; Toyota Carina Mk1; Toyota Celica; Toyota Corona; Toyota Cressida; Toyota Hi-Lux 4X4; Toyota Landcruiser; Toyota MR2; Toyota Supra; Triumph 1300; Triumph GT6; Triumph Herald; Triumph Spitfire; Triumph Vitesse.

Vauxhall Astra Mk1; Vauxhall Cavalier Mk1; Vauxhall Cavalier Mk2; Vauxhall Firenza; Vauxhall Nova; Vauxhall Royale; Vauxhall Velox; Vauxhall Viva HC; Volkswagen Golf Mk1; Volkswagen Golf Mk2; Volkswagen Jetta Mk2; Volkswagen Scirocco.

Low Risk

Alfa Romeo 33; Aston Martin; Audi 80; Audi 100 Mk1; Audi 100 Mk2; Audi 200; Austin Allegro Mk1/2; Austin Allegro Mk3; Austin/Morris A30–135; Austin/Morris Ambassador; Austin/Morris Maxi; Austin/Morris Princess; Bentley (all ranges); BMW 500 series (E34); BMW 700 series (E32); Citroën 2 CV; Citroën AX; Citroën BX; Citroën CX; Citroën Dyane; Citroën GS/GSA; Citroën Visa; Citroën XM.

DAF (all ranges); Daihatsu Charade Mk1; Daihatsu Charade Mk2; Daihatsu Charmant; Daimler Double-Six; Fiat 126; Fiat 127; Fiat 128; Fiat Panda Mk1; Fiat Panda Mk2; Fiat Regata Mk1; Fiat Regata Mk2; Fiat Strada Mk3; Fiat Tipo; Fiat Uno

Mk1; Fiat Uno Mk2; Fiat X1/9; Ford Anglia/Prefect; FSO (all ranges); General Motors USA (all ranges); Hillman Hunter; Hillman Imp; Honda Accord; Honda Ballade; Honda Civic; Honda Concerto; Honda Legend; Honda Prelude; Humber (all ranges); Hyundai Pony Mk1; Hyundai Pony Mk2; Hyundai Stellar.

Jensen (all ranges); Lada 1200; Lada 1500; Lada 1600; Lada Niva; Lada Riva; Lada Samara; Lancia Prisma; Lancia Y10 Mk1; Landrover 88; Landrover 90; Landrover 109; Landrover 110; Lotus Esprit/Elan; Mazda 121; Mazda 323 Mk1; Mazda 323 Mk2; Mazda 626 Mk1; Mazda 626 Mk2; Mercedes 190; Mercedes Compacts; Mercedes G-Wagon; Mercedes S Class; Mercedes Sports; MG MGB; Mitsubishi/Colt 1200; Mitsubishi/Colt 1400; Mitsubishi/Colt Galant; Mitsubishi/Colt Tredia; Morgan (all ranges); Morris Ital; Morris Marina.

Nissan/Datsun Bluebird Mk2; Nissan/Datsun Cherry; Nissan/Datsun Laurel; Nissan/Datsun Micra; Nissan/Datsun Prairie; Nissan/Datsun Stanza; Nissan/Datsun Sunny Mk1–4; Nissan/Datsun Sunny Mk5; Opel Monza; Opel Rekord; Peugeot 104; Peugeot 205; Peugeot 305; Peugeot 309; Peugeot 405; Peugeot 505; Proton (all ranges).

Reliant Scimitar; Renault 4; Renault 5 Mk1; Renault 5 Mk2; Renault 9; Renault 11; Renault 12; Renault 14; Renault 16; Renault 18; Renault 19; Renault 20; Renault 21; Renault 25; Renault Espace; Renault Fuego; Rolls Royce; Rover 200 Mk1; Rover 60–110; Rover 800; Saab 9000; Saab 95/96; Saab 99; Seat Ibiza; Seat Malaga; Singer (all ranges); Skoda Estelle Mk1; Skoda Estelle Mk2; Skoda Favorit; Subaru 2WD; Subaru 4WD; Subaru Justy; Sunbeam (all ranges); Suzuki SJ; Suzuki Swift; Suzuki Vitara; Talbot Alpine; Talbot Avenger; Talbot Horizon; Talbot Samba; Talbot Solara; Talbot Sunbeam; Talbot Tagora; Toyota Camry; Toyota Carina Mk2; Toyota Carina Mk3; Toyota Corolla; Toyota Starlet; Toyota Tercel; Triumph 1500; Triumph 2500; Triumph Acclaim; Triumph Dolomite.

Vauxhall Carlton; Vauxhall Cavalier Mk3; Vauxhall Chevette;

Vauxhall Victor/VX; Vauxhall Viva HA/HB; Vauxhall/Opel Senator; Volkswagen Beetle; Volkswagen Derby; Volkswagen Jetta Mk1; Volkswagen Passat; Volkswagen Polo; Volkswagen Santana; Volvo 140; Volvo 160; Volvo 440; Volvo 480; Volvo '200'; Volvo '300'; Volvo '700'; Zastava Yugo.

6. Policing

INTRODUCTION

At no time in its history has the British police service been under so much pressure. The huge crime rises of the last twenty years, the corruption scandals (for example, the Guildford Four, the Birmingham Six), the growing public distrust of those in high positions: all these things have been hard enough to bear. But now a new set of problems has emerged, all centring on one word: reform. The government is putting all parts of the police service under scrutiny. Everything from pay structures and contractual arrangements, to the way clear-up rates are measured, is to be exposed to close examination.

The Sheehy Inquiry, whose report was published in the summer of 1993, is one aspect of this drive towards restructuring the police. Commentators and scrutineers compete to make their own contribution to the debate about policing quality. All sorts of changes are possible, and everything is under discussion, though nothing is certain. Amalgamation of forces, privatizing of certain policing functions, reform of methods of measuring efficiency and crime rates, changes to the rank structure and the balance of ranks within forces, renewed community policing, recruitment of more civilian staff and part-time officers, changes to sentencing and custodial practices, to financial structures, to community liaison groups . . .

The police themselves are unhappy: with their conditions of service, with the conflicting demands of the public, with the weaknesses of the criminal justice system, with sentencing policy, with the increased paperwork and administration that burden them. Matters are worsened by the current government's reputation for muddle and inefficiency. Nobody can be sure that any of the talk will amount to much.

For many members of the public everything surrounding the

police at the moment seems extraordinarily chaotic. In this chapter we do not attempt to be definitive (nobody could be definitive about British policing in its current condition). Instead, in a period of rapid change, we aim to present the reader with some useful ideas about, and approaches to, the subject in the hope that this will help individuals to make their own contributions to arguments about policing. Such arguments are desperately in need of informed, rather than heated, comment.

This chapter also has a more practical role: the more people understand about police structures and issues the better they will be able to ensure they get a reasonable service from their local police. Developing an understanding of modern policing is an essential part of all attempts to guard against crime

Case Study: Police in Revolt

An unprecedented protest against Sir Patrick Sheehy's proposals for police reform brought 20,000 police officers to a rally at Wembley Stadium in the summer of 1993. Not since the police strike of 1919 have police officers voiced such deep and open anger against government. About half the 51 chief constables sent support messages. Speakers at the rally, who included senior figures from the two main opposition parties, vigorously attacked the government and generally described the proposals as crude cost-cutting disguised as reform.

The rally marked the beginning of a massive campaign against the 272 recommendations contained in the government-sponsored Sheehy Report. Proposals which particularly incensed police officers include those given immediately below.

1. Performance related pay systems to be introduced, overtime and annual pay reviews to be scrapped.

2. Recruits to get £2000 less per annum than at present.

3. All officers to be on fixed term contracts, renewable every 5 to 10 years.

4. Unlimited sick leave to be abolished, replaced with a maximum of 6 months on full pay, 6 months on half pay.

5. Several middle to senior ranks to be scrapped, causing 5000 redundancies.

6. Retirement age to be raised from 55 to 60.

These proposals are best seen in the context of a recently released white paper, outlining the government's general thinking. A number of points are emphasized in the document: there should be clearly defined policing priorities, local consultation, local performance targets and strategies, published assessments of performance; there will be job-sharing, part-time working, new shift systems; time spent on paperwork will be reduced; competitive tendering will seek value for money; management will generally be streamlined; there are no immediate plans for force amalgamations, but amalgamation procedures will be simplified, and the Inspectorate of Constabulary will be reinvigorated by people brought in from outside the service.

The general drift is quite clear. Police forces are to be encouraged to imitate cost-cutting private security firms. This, if it is to be accomplished by the target date of 1995, involves a massive set of cultural and procedural changes, not to mention a considerable reduction in police pay and conditions of service. It is not surprising, therefore, that police should start to display the same radical opposition to government that has previously been displayed by such professional groups as teachers. Police officers enjoy greater public support, however, than school teachers, and the government may find itself fighting an even harder battle than that currently being fought over education reform.

Case Study: Vigilantism

While police and politicians fight each other members of the public, increasingly, seem eager to take on the task of fighting criminals. A well-publicized case in Norfolk, in which two men were jailed after they kidnapped an alleged local troublemaker and thief, brought the issue once more into public prominence.

A great deal of media attention was immediately focused on the subject, and this made it hard to determine whether vigilantism had actually risen or whether it was simply that media interest in it had increased.

Nonetheless those claiming that vigilantism had rocketed, because of public disillusionment with the criminal justice system, could point to many examples in support of their case, and there is no doubt that the authorities are worried by the whole question. In 1992, for instance, vigilantes captured a gang of criminals in York; they stormed the homes of alleged murderers in Wales; in London they beat up someone accused of child-molesting; in Hereford they mounted night patrols; in Manchester they threw an alleged wrongdoer in a canal; in Newton, Powys, a group called 'The Twelve Just Men' put ferrets down the trouser legs of alleged local burglars . . .

Some commentators claim that the phenomenon arises out of the Neighbourhood Watch movement, which gave many people the opportunity, for the first time, to become involved in their own policing. The comparative failure of Watches, it is claimed, has persuaded a number of those involved to take things a bit further.

Whatever its causes, the apparent rise in vigilantism is widely seen as a dramatic symbol of precisely how much our system of justice and law enforcement has gone wrong.

POLICE ORGANIZATION

This section is designed to give the reader a basic idea of police institutions, as they currently exist. It is possible that great changes will be made in police organization over the next few years, but it is very difficult at this stage to say exactly what these changes will be. Readers will have a better comprehension of police reforms, and the debate over such reforms, if they have a grasp of the institutional structures that currently exist.

Main Police Forces

There are 51 regional or 'area' police forces in England, Scotland and Wales. The total of officers, excluding civilian staff, is around 125,000 in England and Wales. The corresponding figure in Scotland is about 14,000. Of the forces, 43 are in England and Wales and 8 are in Scotland. Of the English and Welsh forces 41 are often described as 'provincial' (as are 7 of the 8 Scots forces), being distinctly different in size and complexity from London's Metropolitan Police (the remaining force is the City of London, a small and distinctive body which polices London's compact commercial centre). 6 of the so-called provincial forces in England and Wales are more accurately described as 'metropolitan', being considerably larger than the others, and encompassing big urban conurbations. These smaller versions of London's Metropolitan force are: Greater Manchester, Merseyside, Northumbria, South Yorkshire, West Midlands, and West Yorkshire (Strathclyde in Scotland is similar).

Below we look in turn at the regional forces as a whole and then at London's Met.

1. Regional Forces: England, Scotland and Wales

The operational region normally corresponds to that of the county or metropolitan area after which the force is named, although sometimes this is more complicated. The 'catchment' area of the Greater Manchester or Sussex forces is, therefore, self-evident. The West Mercia force, however, covers the county of Shropshire and also Hereford and Worcestershire. Each force is organized into divisions and sub-divisions.

The regional forces are prime candidates for reorganization. Critics have argued for years that there are too many of them, and that this makes co-ordination difficult and needlessly duplicates costs and bureaucracy. Mergers are a possibility, perhaps eventually reducing the number of forces to as few as 20 or so. Critics argue that this will be unwieldy and contrary to the public demand for a more local policing style. It will be some time before this debate is resolved.

2. The Metropolitan Police

The Met is the biggest, most important and most historically significant force in the UK. Its fame spreads worldwide, and with more than 28,000 officers it is larger than many other forces combined. It polices an area within a radius of 15 miles from Central London (excluding the district covered by the City of London Police). It is divided into 8 districts (known formally as Areas), each of which in turn contains its own divisions. The Met's new Commissioner has already announced plans for a major reshaping of the force's structure.

Chain of Command

Police forces have evolved highly complex rank structures. If these are reformed it is hard to say exactly how it will be done. One possibility is that the number of senior officers will be reduced, on the grounds that forces are top-heavy and bureaucratic. The role and importance of the 'constable on the ground' would be correspondingly enhanced. Accordingly the Sheehy Report, released in the summer of 1993, recommends that three ranks – chief inspector, chief superintendent and deputy chief constable – be abolished. This would cause 5,000 redundancies, but 3,000 constables would be recruited. The Sheehy Report is opposed by the great mass of police officers.

In England and Wales the command hierarchy is as follows.

1. Provincial Forces

Chief Constable
Deputy Chief Constable
Assistant Chief Constable
Chief Superintendent
Superintendent
Chief Inspector
Inspector

Sergeant
Constable

2. Metropolitan Police

The Met's command structure is identical to that of other forces, up to and including the rank of Chief Superintendent. Beyond that level the structure is as follows, in descending order of importance.

Commissioner
Deputy Commissioner
Assistant Commissioner
Deputy Assistant Commissioner
Commander

3. City of London Police

Like the Met, the City force has a rank structure which, up to and including the post of Chief Superintendent, is identical to that of provincial forces. Also like the Met, it has its own rank structure for posts senior to Chief Superintendent, and these are given here in descending order of importance.

Commissioner
Assistant Commissioner
Commander

4. Scotland

Scots forces have a command structure which follows that of English and Welsh provincial forces.

Operational Departments

Each force is led by its Chief Constable or Commissioner. Senior officers, below the Chief Constable, control particular departments and types of policing activity. The particular policing region covered by the force is also divided into Areas, Divisions and Sub-Divisions, and these are normally controlled by Superintendents or Chief Superintendents (the Metropolitan force differs slightly from the others in this, given its greater size). Every Area, Division or Sub-Division has its own police stations.

Operational responsibilities, in a typical force, are divided as follows, under the four main categories of Crime, Operations, Traffic, and Management and Training. Each of the four is supervised by a separate senior officer, under the ultimate command of the Chief Constable or Commissioner. Obviously the different departments overlap and in practice there is a lot of organizational variation, depending on operational need.

The allocation of responsibilities, in a typical force, might generally resemble that laid out below.

1. Main Department: Crime

Sub-Departments: a. Special Branch. b. Fingerprints and Photography. c. Fraud Squad.

2. Main Department: Operations

Sub-Departments: a. Task Force. b. Horses, Dogs, Police Boats. c. Communications.

3. Main Department: Traffic

Sub-Departments: a. Road Safety. b. Motorway Patrol. c. Vehicle Testing.

4. Main Department: Management and Training

Sub-Departments: a. Recruitment and Postings. b. Training. c. Buildings.

Specialist Police Units

The major regional forces are not the only police organizations that operate in Britain. There is a considerable range of other police forces and specialist offshoots.

Regional Crime Squads, for example, draw officers from a number of neighbouring forces to tackle major crime. There are various national units which co-ordinate information on everything from drugs to football violence. The Channel Islands have their own forces. The British Transport Police maintain law and order on British Rail and London Transport. The Atomic Energy Authority, the Ministry of Defence, Customs and Excise, the Post Office, the Ministry of Agriculture, the Inland Revenue, and various port authorities are amongst those authorized to run their own police and/or investigation units. People are often surprised to learn that the range of bodies embraced by this category includes such institutions as the Tobacco Advisory Council and British Telecom.

A separate question is the role of private security firms. These are willing to hire out security services, patrolling estates and neighbourhoods. It has been suggested that such companies will become the pace-makers in the field of security and law enforcement in this country. It is too early yet to say whether this sort of activity will make a major impact on British law enforcement, and it raises complex issues about accountability and quality which we do not have the space to explore in this text.

Control of the Police

Restriction of powers has for long been a guiding assumption in the regulation of British policing. This cautionary tradition underlies the apportioning of overall responsibility for policing in each region. A triumvirate, composed of the Home Secretary, Chief Constable, and the local police authority, as defined by the Police Act 1964, controls each force in England and Wales.

However, the Metropolitan Police does not have a police authority and is governed jointly by the Home Secretary and the Commissioner, and the City of London Police has the Common Council of the City as its police authority.

None of the three, at least theoretically, has total authority. Such limitation makes the system of police control a classic example of the unwritten British constitution in application, with its emphasis on checks and balances to preserve maximum freedom, and its distrust of excessive centralization. Perhaps vagueness is both its chief weakness and strength. This allows for considerable flexibility and for adaptability to changing circumstance, but can also generate muddle and inconsistency.

Theoretically, then, the three different parts of the triumvirate are like three men chained together. None can dominate the others: the chains are too restricting. For the same reason none can move without the co-operation of the others: they are forced to seek a balance. Any attempts at constitutional reform are likely to focus on one corner of this triangle: the police authorities, on the grounds that they can be bureaucratic and meddlesome. Their defenders will say that any attempt to curtail them is an assault upon local democracy and accountability. The fluidity and sheer messiness of contemporary public administration in Britain mean that it is impossible to predict the outcome of such a debate.

Scotland

The Scots system is similar to that of England and Wales, except that its forces report to the Scottish Secretary rather than the Home Secretary. Police powers and constitution are governed by different legislation, but the guiding principles are very similar, in most respects, to those in England and Wales.

Police Roles

The Constable

Ordinary police constables are in many ways the most important, as well as the most numerous, components of the police
service. They are the officers whom the public are most likely
to meet. Because of this, police-public relations depend heavily
upon them.

Often they are the very first to arrive at an incident and they
function in the front line, 'taking the flak' for the decisions and
policies of their superiors. This is an increasing cause of stress,
as relations with the public have deteriorated and as society
demands more from the police in general. Much of their work,
however, is mundane: patrolling the streets, answering calls
from the public, dealing with paperwork, supervising public
events and demonstrations. They work also in crown, magistrates and coroners' courts. Sometimes they take on specialist
roles, becoming dog handlers, mounted police, firearms licensing
officers, etc. Others become crime prevention or 'home beat'
patrol officers (although this last role is regarded, unfairly, as
having low status).

They do some minor investigative work concerning offences
such as petty theft, minor assaults and autocrime. Usually they
work to a shift pattern, three shifts often covering 24 hours.

The morale of police constables has possibly never been lower,
despite the considerable improvements in pay and conditions
which they have received over the last fifteen years. They feel
overwhelmed by ever-increasing paperwork, and frustrated by
what they perceive as the contradictory demands of the public
('If we get stuck in to the villains we're criticized,' said one
officer, 'and if we don't intervene and play it down we're
criticized also'). Another cause of complaint is police recruitment policies. Many rank and file PCs resent the privileges
accorded to the special 'fast-track' officers, often graduates, who
are given accelerated promotion. One danger is that such grievances will make many PCs, who do not belong to the favoured
categories, feel like an internal underclass, with subsequent damage to their morale.

The Detective

What detectives actually do is much less exciting than the popular image of their activities suggests. Often diligent filing and fact-checking are far more important, in the process of catching criminals, than clever insights. A great deal depends, also, on the use of informers who often provide the vital bits of data that make arrests possible. The requisite personal skills, in building a network of informants, and in judging the reliability of witnesses, are important to CID officers in general. Much detective work is unstructured and even less predictable than other police activity. This flexibility is a weakness as well as a strength. It allows great scope for initiative. Yet on occasion it tempts officers into the sort of unorthodox behaviour that may rapidly become corrupt.

Each force has its own detective section (the CID or Criminal Investigation Department). Detectives compose about 12% of police personnel and each one is trained in one of half a dozen detective training schools. Rank structures generally follow those of uniformed officers, and the word 'detective' is mostly added to formal titles (e.g. Detective Sergeant').

Civilian Staff

Some of the most crucial people who work in policing are not police officers. A great many functions are in fact performed by civilians, who now number well over 50,000 throughout England, Scotland and Wales. They perform many different administrative, secretarial and technical functions. For instance they prepare legal documents, and monitor court cases; they process accident reports and drink-driving offences; they also carry out forensic and fingerprint examination.

The benefit of this, from a police viewpoint, is that it reduces the time officers spend on routine tasks, so that they can devote more time to 'real policing'. And frequently it is cheaper, as junior administrative staff command lower wages than officers. For these reasons 'civilianization', as it is termed, has been greatly encouraged and has increased considerably over the past decade. It will probably increase further as Chief Constables try to reduce costs and increase efficiency by allowing officers to concentrate on their primary tasks.

POLICE PERFORMANCE

One of the most contentious policing issues is performance measurement. Just how effective are different police forces, and what are the best methods of assessing that effectiveness? In this section we shall examine different performance indicators in turn; although there is no space for exhaustive analysis, we do hope readers will then be better informed about the vital debates concerning police efficiency.

Crime Totals

Which police force areas have recorded the most crime in the last few years? A rank order, covering annual totals for 1986, 1989 and 1991, might look as follows (figures are rounded in thousands and include criminal damage under £20).

1986 rank	Police force	1986 (000s)	1989 (000s) and rank	1991 (000s) and rank
1.	Metropolitan Police	768.5	756.3 (1)	926.2 (1)
2.	Greater Manchester	321.5	294.2 (2)	380.8 (2)
3.	West Midlands	268.0	229.0 (3)	302.8 (3)
4.	West Yorkshire	177.0	188.8 (4)	295.5 (4)
5.	Merseyside	168.7	135.9 (6)	148.8 (10)
6.	Northumbria	164.9	181.6 (5)	226.2 (5)
7.	Thames Valley	118.5	120.7 (7)	187.2 (6)
8.	South Wales	110.0	118.2 (8)	162.0 (7)
9.	Hampshire	96.8	99.4 (11)	143.9 (11)
10.	Nottinghamshire	94.5	105.6 (9)	150.6 (9)
11.	Avon and Somerset	93.6	100.1 (10)	153.8 (8)
12.	South Yorkshire	91.9	94.4 (12)	125.6 (13)

13.	Lancashire	87.1	89.9 (14)	122.5 (14)
14.	Humberside	81.8	91.4 (13)	118.8 (15)
15.	Kent	75.5	83.6 (15)	138.4 (12)
16.	Essex	74.9	77.4 (16)	108.4 (17)
17.	Devon and Cornwall	72.5	77.0 (17)	108.2 (18)
18.	Sussex	67.7	75.5 (18)	112.2 (16)
19.	Cleveland	58.1	60.8 (19)	78.1 (21)
20.	Staffordshire	57.0	59.4 (20)	86.3 (20)
21.	West Mercia	52.3	52.5 (22)	74.2 (23)
22.	Leicestershire	49.0	54.8 (21)	89.8 (19)
23.	Cheshire	47.3	47.9 (24)	66.3 (24)
24.	Derbyshire	46.5	48.8 (23)	75.6 (22)
25.	Durham	44.5	46.1 (25)	65.2 (25)
26.	Hertfordshire	43.0	41.8 (27)	55.6 (31)
27.	Norfolk	40.1	44.6 (26)	64.1 (26)
28.	Bedfordshire	39.3	40.9 (28)	57.1 (29)
29.	Northamptonshire	38.3	39.0 (30)	58.5 (27)
30.	Dorset	36.8	39.8 (29)	51.6 (32)
31.	North Yorkshire	36.0	35.8 (32)	51.5 (33)
32.	North Wales	35.3	34.7 (35)	44.4 (37)
33.	Surrey	32.9	33.8 (36)	50.1 (34)
34.	Cambridgeshire	32.7	36.9 (31)	58.2 (28)
35.	Lincolnshire	31.5	35.5 (33)	44.9 (36)
36.	Cumbria	30.2	28.2 (38)	45.1 (35)
37.	Suffolk	30.1	32.0 (37)	39.9 (39)
38.	Gloucestershire	29.7	35.2 (34)	56.0 (30)
39.	Wiltshire	28.6	27.7 (39)	39.3 (40)
40.	Gwent	26.6	25.3 (41)	38.7 (41)
41.	Warwickshire	22.8	25.4 (40)	40.5 (38)
42.	Dyfed-Powys	17.8	17.7 (42)	26.0 (42)
43.	City of London	7.8	7.1 (43)	7.6 (43)
Yearly crime totals (000s):		1986	1989	1991
		3847	3870	5276

What can we learn about police performance from such a table? One lesson is that, despite the huge increases in recorded crime, there seems to be little variation, with one or two remarkable exceptions, in the rank order. Most forces in 1991 were in roughly the same position in the table as in 1986.

The other immediately obvious factor is that forces in the top ten all have large populations, and large police forces. Maybe then this kind of table simply tells us what we already know: that where there are more people there is more recorded crime. Of course the raw figures themselves do not explain why Gloucestershire, which has a slightly smaller population than Suffolk, should record so much more per capita crime, for example.

The general point seems to hold: simple bulk comparisons of the amount of crime tell us very little, on their own, about police performance. They tell us that most crime is recorded where there are most people and that there are exceptions to that rule. Such information may be of some initial use when the government is deciding how to allocate resources. Yet in isolation it reveals little about the efficiency with which those resources, once allocated, are used.

Per Capita Crime

Another approach is to look at per capita crime rates, dividing the crime rate by the number of people in the area, to work out the number of recorded crimes per person.

This gives an additional table. The forces are in rank order: forces with the highest per capita crime rates are at the top of the order. The figure after each force gives the average number of crimes per 100 people. The figures are rounded. Because of this, one or two forces will appear to have the same score, even though their 'real' score is slightly different. Their exact score determines their rank position.

PER CAPITA CRIME RATES, ENGLAND AND WALES 1991
(Figures include criminal damage under £20)

1. Northumbria 15.8
2. Nottinghamshire 14.8
3. Greater Manchester 14.7
4. West Yorkshire 14.3
5. Cleveland 14.1
6. Humberside 13.8
7. London Metropolitan 12.9
8. South Wales 12.4
9. West Midlands 11.6
10. Durham 10.9
11. Avon and Somerset 10.9
12. Bedfordshire 10.7
13. Gloucestershire 10.5
14. Merseyside 10.3
15. Northamptonshire 10.1
16. Leicestershire 10.0
17. South Yorkshire 9.7
18. Thames Valley 9.4
19. Cumbria 9.2
20. Kent 9.1
21. Lancashire 8.8
22. Cambridgeshire 8.8
23. Gwent 8.6
24. Hampshire 8.6
25. Norfolk 8.5
26. Warwickshire 8.4
27. Staffordshire 8.3
28. Derbyshire 8.1
29. Sussex 7.9
30. Dorset 7.8
31. Lincolnshire 7.6
32. Essex 7.4
33. Devon and Cornwall 7.2
34. North Yorkshire 7.1
35. Wiltshire 7.0

36. Cheshire 6.9
37. West Mercia 6.9
38. North Wales 6.8
39. Surrey 6.7
40. Hertfordshire 6.6
41. Suffolk 6.2
42. Dyfed-Powys 5.5

(Note: for these purposes the City of London force is included in the figures for London Metropolitan)

These figures offer more precise comparisons, based on, but not to the same extent limited by, the figures for total crime in an area. With this counting method it is possible for big forces to record lower crime frequencies than small forces. Yet seven of the forces in the top ten are also in the first ten in the 1991 table based solely on the total amount of crime per force (Northumbria, Nottinghamshire, Greater Manchester, West Yorkshire, London Metropolitan, South Wales, West Midlands).

The three newcomers to the first ten are all from impoverished though not especially populous areas in the north-east (Cleveland, Humberside, Durham) and two of them, Cleveland and Durham, are respectively 16 and 15 places higher than in the 1991 bulk crime ranking. Dyfed-Powys comes bottom of both the tables for total amount of crime and per capita crime, and both Suffolk and North Wales are in roughly the same places at the bottom of both rankings.

Yet apart from the top and bottom ends, there is considerable variation between the two tables: 25 of the 51 forces vary by more than five places in their position in the two rankings. The merits of the two tables, one offering crime totals, and the other per capita rates, could be argued either way. Yet there is little doubt that per capita crime rates offer a more precise judgement of recorded crime rates.

But the central word here, as with all official figures, is 'recorded'. It may be that these figures simply indicate the willingness, or unwillingness, in particular regions, of the police to record crime and of the public to report it. There may well be a great amount of crime in a particular area that is not reported

and recorded, or that is reported but not recorded because of
strict police interpretation of the rules; or it may even be that
a zealous force and vigilant populace are reporting an unusually
high proportion of the crime that occurs in a force area.

So recorded crime rates in isolation can tell us about only one
thing with certainty: the extent of police recording activity and
of public reporting to the police. These are not inconsiderable
things; they take up a great deal of police time and are therefore
relevant to considerations of police efficiency. But they do not
tell us with certainty about the full extent of crime in a region,
nor about what the police are doing to prevent and hinder criminal activity. Of course in actuality the figures are not interpreted
in isolation. Nobody is surprised by the news that high per
capita crime rates often occur in police areas with high concen-
trations of urban poverty and youth unemployment.

Existing crime figures are of great interest, then, provided
we handle them with appropriate care and knowledge of their
limitations. But, for measurements of police efficiency, as
opposed to activity, other indexes are required.

Clear-Up Rates

Clear-up rates are performance indicators which will be looked
at very closely in the coming period. Yet they have serious weaknesses. In the first place a cleared-up crime is by no means
necessarily an offence for which someone has been found guilty
in a court. Nor does it necessarily even signify that someone has
been charged with a crime. A 'clear-up' can be a wide variety
of things, including a summons, a caution or of course a charge
or a conviction. This notorious wideness of definition has led
in the past to some serious book-cooking. Forces that were strict
about what they called a clear-up were, in this manner, made
to look bad by less scrupulous forces eager to record everything
they could as a clear-up. The London Met, for instance, has
often recorded a much lower clear-up rate than others, simply
because its working definition of a cleared-up crime has been

fairly narrow (clear-up rates across the country have been falling for some years, and are usually in the thirty to forty per cent range – see the Glossary for the official definition of a 'clear-up').

Crimes taken into consideration, and confessed by prisoners in cells, in return for judicial leniency, are also eligible. Abuse of this in the past, by which criminals were persuaded to confess to crimes they had not committed, to boost police clear-up rates, led to recent tightening up of the rules governing this sort of clear up and its classification.

A number of people favour the division of clear-ups into primary or secondary, to give a more detailed idea of what is actually happening in a force (primary clear-ups would be those involving a charge or formal caution). But even this would be open to abuse: some forces could record lots of minor offences to push their figures up, compared to other forces which might actually clear up fewer but more important offences, and this would not be revealed in the figures, so long as these minor offences led to a charge or caution.

More elaborate ways of classifying clear-ups could easily be devised, but these would then be getting away from the immediacy and clarity which people seek in performance indicators. Clear-ups, in many ways, illustrate the difficulties facing those trying to find straightforward indexes of police efficiency.

Arrest Rates

Despite giant recorded crime rises in the last few years there is considerable evidence that many police forces are arresting fewer people, or that the number of arrests is stable, and that police bring a smaller proportion of those they do arrest to court. Critics of the police say this is yet more evidence of inefficiency and lack of zeal.

Police themselves blame lack of resources in a period of great pressure upon them. Police officers contend, privately, that they are discouraged from making arrests, particularly in the case of the juveniles who commit a great deal of crime. 'You can put all that time and effort into nicking them and then they get off with a slap on the wrist. Or the Crown Prosecution Service decides not to go ahead with the case. In any case there's a lot of pressure on us to let them off with a formal caution.' This last point is causing increasing disquiet. Recently, the government has encouraged the use of formal cautions as an alternative to prosecutions, to take the heat off an overloaded criminal justice system. This further discourages the police, who feel it makes a travesty of attempts to control crime: 'A formal caution is no deterrent.' Police are also unhappy about the Police and Criminal Evidence Act. This act, which was brought in because of police abuses of rules of custody and evidence, means that police must go through more intensive pre-trial work and it makes it harder for them to get disclosures from suspects. They claim it is a disincentive both to making arrests and to bringing charges post-arrest. 'Effectively we've gone on a work to rule' said one officer. 'We just don't bother a lot of the time.'

Whatever the causes behind the falling arrest rate, to the public it is bewildering. It seems that fewer people are going to court and being punished just at a point when the need for court proceedings has never seemed greater. However, there are strong indications that the current review of the criminal justice system will address some of the grievances that make police reluctant to pursue criminals.

Below are given tables for the percentage change in arrests in 1991, in England and Wales, and also the average number of arrests per officer. The figures included many 'non-indictable' minor offences which are not normally included in recorded crime figures. Forces appear in rank order of arrests per officer. The figures are provisional. Those for London Met are collected differently from the others.

	Arrests per officer	Change in arrest totals
1991		
Nottinghamshire	20	2%
Cleveland	19	6%
Hampshire	19	−1%
Lancashire	19	8%

Lincolnshire	19	6%
Northumbria	19	4%
West Midlands	19	6%
Cumbria	18	9%
Durham	18	−3%
Humberside	18	−1%
North Wales	18	8%
South Wales	18	3%
Staffordshire	18	6%
Greater Manchester	17	0
Northamptonshire	17	6%
Bedfordshire	16	−1%
Cheshire	16	7%
Kent	16	2%
Thames Valley	16	1%
West Yorkshire	16	2%
Gwent	15	4%
Merseyside	15	5%
Norfolk	15	−8%
North Yorkshire	15	3%
South Yorkshire	15	4%
West Mercia	15	−1%
Cambridgeshire	14	−4%
Dorset	14	5%
Dyfed-Powys	14	6%
Essex	14	0
Gloucestershire	14	0
Hertfordshire	14	2%
Leicestershire	14	6%
Warwickshire	14	7%
Avon and Somerset	13	−8%
Derbyshire	13	3%
Suffolk	13	13%
Sussex	13	5%
Wiltshire	12	−6%
Devon and Cornwall	12	8%
Surrey	12	−5%
City of London	6	−3%
Metropolitan	4	−3%

Any set of crime figures which asesses only one or two years in isolation must be interpreted with caution. Such figures are used here purely by way of illustration, and are not regarded as being definitive in themselves. Nonetheless, these statistics may point to a problem, especially when linked to anecdotal evidence of police disillusionment and declining court-room activity around the country.

The fact remains that some forces have a markedly different arrest rate from others. Nottingham police total 20 arrests per officer. Forces at the other end of the scale arrest far fewer people. Is this an index of inefficiency, of an unwillingness to get out on the street and do the real job? Or is it evidence of over-zealousness on the part of Nottinghamshire's constabulary? Or does it merely reflect different operational or even recording policies, with some forces concentrating on the more serious crimes and adopting a low-key attitude in sensitive inner-city areas? Or are certain officers even more disillusioned and demoralized than others, even more weighed down by the feeling that the whole system works against them?

Twelve forces recorded a decline in numbers of arrests, including Cambridgeshire, which also experienced a 31% increase in recorded crime (including offences of criminal damage under £20 in value). Another three forces showed no change in arrest totals. An additional eleven forces recorded arrest total increases of less than 5%. Only one force, Suffolk, increased its arrest rate by double figures: 13% This was a long way ahead of its nearest rival and in a year when the average recorded crime increase in England and Wales, including criminal damage below £20, was 16% (the figures do not completely match: the total number of arrests includes all arrests for all offences; recorded crime figures exclude a large number of small 'non-indictable' offences).

Whatever the reason, the fact that arrest rates are dropping, while the country seems gripped by ever-rising crime, means that the current governmental review of the system is even more important. Indications are that the fall in arrest rates has not gone unnoticed at the highest governmental levels.

Finance

Is finance a good way of measuring police efficiency? The idea has a hard-nosed attractiveness but may present problems. The most immediately obvious method of applying such analysis is to measure the cost per officer. This can then be cross-referenced with other indicators, such as crime rates.

However, different accounting methods and administrative practices may make comparisons difficult. High costs may be nothing more than an index of particular accountancy techniques, and may to an extent simply reflect the fact that some parts of the country, for reasons unrelated to policing, are intrinsically more expensive than others. Nonetheless, given the importance of money in our lives, finance is obviously worth looking at in assessments of police performance. Below in alphabetical order we present costs per officer for the 43 English and Welsh forces (Scots figures were not available at time of writing). The figures are provided by the Chartered Institute of Public Finance and Accountancy (CIPFA).

ESTIMATED EXPENDITURE PER POLICE OFFICER 1992–93

Non-Metropolitan England	Net Expenditure £000s
Avon and Somerset	39,681
Bedfordshire	37,854
Cambridgeshire	40,530
Cheshire	38,325
Cleveland	37,962
Cumbria	40,722
Derbyshire	41,437
Devon and Cornwall	43,022
Dorset	43,460
Durham	37,393
Essex	42,157
Gloucestershire	41,338
Hampshire	41,242
Hertfordshire	41,222

Humberside	40,250
Kent	42,442
Lancashire	39,530
Leicestershire	39,319
Lincolnshire	41,095
Norfolk	41,344
Northamptonshire	43,141
North Yorkshire	40,592
Nottinghamshire	38,805
Staffordshire	39,590
Suffolk	41,018
Surrey	39,695
Sussex	36,964
Thames Valley	42,600
Warwickshire	42,674
West Mercia	41,070
Wiltshire	38,649

Wales

Dyfed-Powys	40,225
Gwent	39,299
North Wales	40,284
South Wales	39,327

English Metropolitan

Greater Manchester	39,631
Merseyside	40,571
Northumbria	39,562
South Yorkshire	37,920
West Midlands	39,958
West Yorkshire	42,233

London

City	56,735
Metropolitan	51,651

The obvious immediate qualification to make is that this table only covers one financial year. Figures provided may not be typical and can be affected by extraordinary factors in any one year. To get a really accurate picture figures for several years would be necessary. However the totals still provide some interesting results. The two most expensive forces, on this evidence, are those in London. This is perhaps not surprising given London's higher costs, but why is the tiny City force so much more expensive, per officer, than its giant neighbour?

Analysing the totals for non-metropolitan forces we find that the most expensive are Northants and Dorset, both of which are relatively low-crime areas, compared to crime-ridden Cleveland which is considerably cheaper. Sussex is the lowest spender at £36,964 per officer. Non-metropolitan forces, which are comparatively expensive, include Warwickshire, Suffolk, Kent, Hampshire, Essex and Gloucestershire. Spenders below this level include Lancashire, Durham, Avon and Somerset, Nottinghamshire and Wiltshire.

The problem is: which is cause and which effect? For instance, is Cleveland's per capita crime rate high because its costs per officer are low? Or are costs low simply because of low resourcing? Or, alternatively, is it a sign of efficiency that high-crime Cleveland keeps its costs lower than nearby Northumbria which has a higher per capita crime rate and spends about £1600 more per officer? Or are Northumbria's costs higher than Cleveland's simply because it faces more problems and has more crime to fight? And what about Durham, adjacent to both of them, and yet boasting the lowest costs per officer and much lower crime rates?

All sorts of interpretations are possible and we are obviously still at an early stage in analysing such data. Many other permutations are feasible, comparing arrest rates to finance figures, for example. It is however useful to look at such figures even in their raw state. Finance is one of the major factors in government decision-making. Familiarity with the costs of your local policing helps you assess the sort of service you can expect from local law enforcement systems.

Scotland

Most of our police performance data, because of availability, is for England and Wales. To place this in perspective we also provide, below, some Scots figures.

RECORDED CRIME TOTALS, AND PER CAPITA CRIME RATES PER 100 PEOPLE, SCOTLAND, 1992.
(Per capita figures are rounded)

	Recorded crime totals	Per 100 people
Central	23,042	8.4
Dumfries and Galloway	10,586	7.2
Fife	34,641	10
Grampian	42,842	8.3
Lothian and Borders	95,462	11.2
Northern	13,756	5
Strathclyde	318,703	13.9
Tayside	50,529	12.9
Per capita average, Scotland		11.6

Victim Surveys

Victim surveys, in which crime victims are interviewed and asked about their experiences of crime, provide considerable insights into crime recording and law enforcement processes. The major surveys, like the British Crime Survey, claim to detect a lot of crime that is not reported to police. Much of this unreported and unrecorded crime is however not reported because its victims do not think it sufficiently serious. Crime surveys also have methodological weaknesses, as does all opinion-based research, but they have considerable potential in the measurement of police performance. However they have not reached the stage whereby they are consistently available on a regional basis, so they cannot yet provide us with consistent indexes of comparative police performance across the country. Potentially they could be of great benefit in this respect, once the expense and complexity of implementing them are addressed (see the information about the British Crime Survey under Crime Risks).

SERVICE PROVISION

We now look at the practicalities of dealing directly with the police. What sort of service are they supposed to provide? What questions do you ask in assessing whether they provide it? How do you proceed if you wish to become more involved in influencing local policing? We also look at rights on arrest: sometimes an individual's only contact with the police is when they are conducting an investigation, and it is important, for all involved, including the police, that proper procedures are followed. The complaints procedure, an essential means of redress, is explained in some detail.

Statement of Intent

In 1990 the Association of Chief Police Officers published a statement of intent. It encapsulates central assumptions that senior police officers claim to make about their work, and provides a starting point for those who wish to assess the quality of service they receive from their local force. It is reproduced in full. The second and third paragraphs, with their emphasis on compassion, sensitivity and openness to change, are particularly important as indexes of the way in which police officers wish to be regarded.

ACPO Strategic Policy Document: Statement of Common Purpose

'The purpose of the Police Service is to uphold the law fairly and firmly: to prevent crime; to pursue and bring to justice those who break the law; to keep the Queen's Peace; to protect, help and reassure the community; and to be seen to do all this with integrity, common sense and sound judgement.

'We must be compassionate, courteous and patient, acting without fear or favour or prejudice to the rights of others. We need to be professional, calm and restrained in the face of violence and apply only that force which is necessary to accomplish our lawful duty.

'We must strive to reduce the fears of the public and, so far as we can, to reflect their priorities in the action we take. We must respond to well-founded criticism with a willingness to change.'

Delivery of Service

Below is a checklist of points to cover when you encounter the police. The encounter may be personal, or it may be impersonal, especially if you become a police station lay visitor or a member of a police community liaison group. We cover personal dealings with the police first, then formal contact with them.

The aim of the points and questions listed is to help the reader identify crucial areas of concern and interest in assessing police activity. A constructive approach is best. The police, like other groups, respond most to advice and criticism that are delivered in a positive spirit. It also does no harm at all to acknowledge and draw attention to areas of police performance that are praiseworthy.

Personal Contact

These pointers are listed to help you get a better service from, and liaison with, the police.

1. If you become a crime victim ensure you know the name and contact details of the officer handling your case.

2. Find out what has been done about your particular problem. You have a right to know what, if anything, is happening on your behalf.

3. If you get an inadequate answer to requests for such information, take the matter to a higher level within the police service. If this fails raise the issue with your local police consultative committee, directly with the police authority, or with a local councillor or another figure in the community, depending on the urgency of the matter.

Ask yourself the following questions. Acting on them or even just reflecting on or communicating them may, in the long term, help both you and the police.

1. Did police respond promptly when you contacted them?

2. Were police officers polite to you? Did they listen to what you said?

3. Did they communicate clearly?
4. Do you feel they gave you prompt and adequate information?

5. Do you know of any police/community consultation groups in your neighbourhood, and have you considered joining them?

6. Do you think your local police are too bureaucratic?

7. Have police, in dealing with you, followed the formal performance objectives laid down in the Chief Constable's report or the Inspectorate of Constabulary report for their area?

8. Have you tried to praise police officers when they behave efficiently and caringly (doing this reinforces good practice)?

Formal Contact

Thinking about the following matters helps you to analyse the kind of service you get from your local police. This is the first step towards doing something about improving the service they offer you.

1. Are police often seen patrolling on local streets?

2. Are they easy to contact by telephone?

3. Do they operate a victim support scheme?

4. What are the formal figures for complaints against police in your area?

5. Are they using good and up-to-date information technology, with computers that actually work and can liaise properly with outside information systems?

6. What percentage of local officers are university graduates?

7. What are the local crime, arrest and complaints rates?

8. Are the annual Chief Constable and Inspectorate of Constabulary reports easy to obtain?

9. Do police make a serious attempt to recruit, on merit, from all sectors of the community?

10. Is there a co-ordinated attempt to provide community policing?

11. Do police try to stay in proper contact with the local public, and are formal consultation and lay visitor schemes efficient and active?

12. Is clear and intelligible information provided about finance and costs per officer?

Getting Involved

Concern at the poor state of police-public relations led to the establishment in the 1980s of several structures designed to make dialogue between police and public a little easier. After the Police and Criminal Evidence Act of 1984, consultative commmittees and lay visitor schemes were initiated.

These initiatives give those interested the chance to assess police performance, and to contribute to debates about police policy and quality. Below we look at them in turn.

Police Community Consultative Committees

These groups vary considerably in the details of their composition and functioning. Usually, however, they are composed of individuals from the police, the police authority, council and voluntary groups. Meetings are usually open to the public and might, on average, be held every couple of months. The committees are obliged to assemble regularly and to maintain proper records.

Often meetings are held at different venues in the locality, giving as many people as possible the chance to participate. Police present reports, committee members raise topics of concern, and anybody else may ask questions or raise issues from the floor of the meeting.

Police often feel that these committees provide valuable ways of defusing problems in the community. However sometimes there has been political opposition. Some voluntary police 'monitoring' groups refuse to participate, and claim that the committees are purely cosmetic and of limited use to the communities they should serve.

Those who wish to become involved should enquire at their local police headquarters.

Lay Visitor Schemes

Lay visitors are able to visit police stations without warning. Their role is to check that stringent conditions, concerning the rights of those detained by police, are followed. These conditions are determined by the Police and Criminal Evidence Act and also by Home Office custody guidelines or rules. Each scheme is the responsibility of the appropriate police authority (in the London Metropolitan area responsibility for the schemes is taken by the Commissioner).

Those interested in participating should apply for details to their local police authority (or to the Commissioner in the London Metropolitan area).

Your Rights on Arrest
by Rita Goddard

Custody rights in England and Wales are determined by the Police and Criminal Evidence Act 1984. In Scotland the equivalent legislation is the Criminal Justice Act 1980. The relevant provisions, made by both these acts, are in practice roughly similar. This is despite the general differences between Scottish and English law. The main practical difference between the two custody systems is in length of detention allowed without charge (see below for details).

In practice your enforceable rights against the police are very limited, and they may even present evidence against you in court which they have obtained illegally.

Nonetheless, remember that you do have certain rights on arrest. If you find yourself taken into police custody it is important to know what they are. Your rights, together with other advice that may prove useful, are summarized below. All points apply throughout the UK, unless indicated otherwise.

Useful Points to Remember

1. Anything you say, however innocent, can be used against you. You are not obliged to say anything, except to give your name, and address (if the police suspect you of having committed an offence, refusing to give this information provides grounds for arrest), to write anything or to sign any statement. Anyone

suspected of being a minor should also give their age. Otherwise, when questioned you have the right to remain silent and it may be in your interest to do so.

2. Stand your ground, but remember that if you appear totally uncooperative the police may feel less likely to respond in a reasonable way towards you.

3. You may be tempted to make up something in the hope it will get you out of trouble. Don't. Remember, everything you say is noted down and when the truth comes out any false information you have given can be used as evidence against you.

4. Make sure you are told why you have been stopped, detained or arrested.

5. If in doubt, say nothing until you have contacted your solicitor or Release, the national drugs and legal helpline.

6. As soon as you can, make notes of what has happened to give to your solicitor including, in the case of uniformed officers, their number should you feel you may need it later. You can use these notes as evidence in court. If you have suffered injury see a doctor as soon as possible, giving a full explanation of your injuries.

7. In England and Wales you cannot usually be held for more than 24 hours without being charged (although an officer of superintendent rank or above may extend this up to 36 hours). However, in the case of a serious arrestable offence (see point 3 below) this may be extended for up to 96 hours. In Scotland, except for suspected terrorist offences, when the same regulations apply as in the rest of the UK (see below), you may not be held for more than 6 hours without charge.

If you are taken to a Police Station

1. You should be made aware of your rights and the legislation governing detention.

2. You have the right to have someone informed if you are arrested, for example a friend.

3. If you are arrested, you have the right to consult a lawyer, or a duty solicitor, who is impartial. This service is provided free of charge. (Should you, however, later find you require representation in court, you would have to either finance this yourself or obtain help, where appropriate, under the legal aid scheme.) If the police suspect you of involvement in a serious arrestable offence, for example supplying drugs or aggravated burglary, they can deny access to a lawyer and refuse to allow you to contact anybody for up to 36 hours. If you are suspected of a terrorist offence the police have the right to hold you incommunicado and without access to a lawyer for up to 48 hours.

4. A note should be made of the time your detention begins. Ensure this is done.

If you are Stopped on the Street

1. Check police identity and ask to see their warrant cards: remember important details, including, in the case of uniformed officers, their numbers.

2. Should you be stopped in the street, ask why. The police may stop you if they have reasonable grounds for suspecting that you have committed or are committing an offence, for example if they believe you have stolen goods in your possession.

3. You are obliged to give your name and other personal details, as mentioned above.

The Police Complaints Authority

Those who consider that they have not received the quality of police service to which they are entitled, or who feel they have been actively maltreated by the police, can make a formal complaint. The main body with responsibility for this process is the Police Complaints Authority (the PCA).

The PCA: Basic Functions

The PCA is completely independent of the police, and is funded separately from them. It was established under the terms of the Police and Criminal Evidence Act, 1984. Its role is to ensure that complaints brought against the police, by members of the public, are always attended to fairly and comprehensively. Its area of responsibility is England and Wales. (The procedure is different in Scotland, and is described at the end of this section.)

No member of the PCA is or has been a police officer. Its chairman is appointed by the Crown. Other members of the authority are appointed by the Home Secretary, who has the power, on a variety of grounds, to remove them. The PCA's two chief functions, in its own words, are to 'supervise the investigation of serious complaints against any police officer involving, for example, death, serious injury or corruption,' and to have 'the final say in deciding whether a police officer should be charged with a breach of discipline.'

Investigation

The Authority is entitled, if it desires, to supervise any complaint against the police that is under investigation. In practice there are two types of investigation. There are certain serious alleged offences whose investigation the PCA is obliged to supervise; other investigations are supervised by the PCA at its own discretion.

1. The PCA must supervise the investigation if it is alleged that a police officer has killed or seriously injured a person.

2. The PCA is always informed, as soon as possible, of allegations that an officer has committed a serious criminal offence. The PCA then decides whether to supervise the investigation.

3. The PCA is particularly interested in supervising investi-

gations 'when they consider it in the public interest to do so'.

4. The PCA may respond to direct requests, from senior police officers or the relevant police authority, to supervise an investigation.

5. The PCA assesses the report detailing each investigation into a complaint against a police officer, regardless of whether or not it supervises the investigation.

Supervision

1. A member of the PCA is given responsibility for each case that the PCA supervises.

2. The PCA has the final say in the appointment of the investigating senior police officer. This officer may be from the force concerned or from another force, depending on circumstance.

3. The PCA member examines the evidence for the complaint and any data relating to the case and then decides how the investigation should be carried out.

4. The member may visit places relevant to the complaint, may observe interviews, may recommend or command that various procedures are pursued.

5. A report, at the end of the investigation, is submitted to the member. The PCA must be satisfied that the investigation has been adequate.

After Investigation

1. It is important to remember that the PCA, whether or not it has supervised the case, assesses the report of every investigation into police complaints.

2. If criminal offences have been committed the chief investigating officer may send the files to the Crown Prosecution Service

(CPS). If this has not been done, then the PCA may insist that it is done. The CPS, which is independent of the police and the PCA, decides whether to prosecute.

3. Where no law seems to have been broken the chief officer concerned must assess whether a disciplinary offence has occurred; the same officer must decide on appropriate measures, if such an offence has been committed, and the PCA assesses these when they are forwarded with the investigation report.

4. The PCA may insist that a disciplinary charge is brought, even if the chief investigating officer does not. The police officer concerned in the complaint is, as a result, summoned to appear before a disciplinary hearing. The hearing may just involve the investigating chief officer, or his deputy, or there may be a tribunal which includes PCA members.

5. If a disciplinary charge is brought the complainant is told and will be able to attend the disciplinary hearing.

6. The PCA will write to the complainant, explaining the reasons, if it decides disciplinary charges are unnecessary. The complainant will be informed if the police officer has been 'advised' or 'warned' about his conduct.

7. This letter from the PCA giving the case outcome is usually the last stage in the whole process.

Civil Proceedings

Those making complaints retain the right to bring court actions concerning their complaint. If a civil action is brought simultaneously with a formal complaint this may slow the formal complaints procedure. The complaints procedure could be delayed, pending the result of the court action. Our courts are not known for speed and the wait could be lengthy and frustrating.

Police officers also are entitled to bring civil actions, if false accusations have maliciously been brought against them. Get legal advice, or speak to your nearest Citizens Advice Bureau, before taking legal action.

Making a Complaint

Before making a complaint you must first decide exactly what it is you are complaining about. Rudeness, damage to property, gratuitous physical harm: these, amongst other things, are grounds for complaint.

The person making the complaint may choose another person to put their case for them. The representative needs written permission from the person they speak for.

Remember, before writing down your complaint, that the police are obliged to enforce the law. The complaints procedure is not designed for those who have a grievance against a particular law. It is relevant to the way in which police apply a law, or set of laws, not to the rightness or wrongness of such laws (other avenues are open to those who desire legal changes).

Write your complaint with great care. It should describe the incidents complained about in detail. It should say:

1. What happened.

2. When it happened.

3. Who was involved.

4. Where it happened.

5. What was said by the participants.

6. Whether there were witnesses.

7. Where witnesses might be contacted.

8. Whether there is evidence, apart from witness evidence, to corroborate the complaint.

When a full written account has been prepared it can be sent to:

1. The Chief Constable of the force concerned.

2. The local police authority of the force concerned, if the officer's rank is above chief superintendent; the Metropolitan Police have no police authority, and such complaints can go to the Commissioner of the Met.

3. If you are unsure about where your complaint should be sent you can simply forward it to the Chief Constable or police authority in your area (their addresses will be in libraries and/ or telephone directories); they will ensure it reaches the proper destination.

4. An officer of your local police station will take the details of your case and pass them on.

5. Local solicitors or advice centres will help you to decide about making a complaint.

6. Complaints may be made direct, in writing, to the Police Complaints Authority, 10 Great George Street, London SW1P 3AE. They will forward complaints to the proper places.

Responses to Complaints

1. Apology: the officer or his force may apologize to you.

2. Explanation: the police may provide justification for the behaviour complained about, so that you decide to withdraw your complaint.

3. Investigation: investigation formally begins, and the PCA becomes directly responsible, if neither of these informal methods of resolving the matter is adequate. The first step is taken when the police appoint a senior officer to lead the investigation. He will take statements from all involved and from there will proceed.

Complaints Procedure in Scotland
by Rita Goddard

Criminal Offences

An alleged criminal offence committed by a police officer must initially be reported to the Procurator Fiscal.

If you are claiming a police officer's behaviour has caused you serious loss or distress, you are advised to consult a solicitor with a view to possible civil court action against the Chief Constable for damages. In such cases you are far likelier to achieve a satisfactory outcome by pursuing legal action for damages in a court than by using the police complaints procedure.

Lesser Offences

1. You may lodge an official complaint personally at any police station. Alternatively, as soon as practicable after the alleged offence has taken place, you should send a written statement detailing your complaint to the Chief Constable for the appropriate region. This is probably the best course of action to take. Give as much information as possible. (See Making a Complaint in England and Wales, points 1. to 8., for guidance).

2. The Deputy Chief Constable will be informed of your complaint and, where the charge is of a non-criminal nature, will appoint a senior police officer to investigate. An interview will be arranged at a police station, or a solicitor's office or your home, if you prefer. You may have a friend present.

3. At the interview you will be asked to make a detailed statement. Check it thoroughly, ensuring that it is a true record of what you have said, with no omissions or deletions. Ensure the police have details of any witnesses you wish to be interviewed.

4. On completion of the investigation the officer responsible will send a report to the Deputy Chief Constable. This is a confidential document; you will not be allowed to see it.

5. You will be notified of the result of the investigation. Should your complaint be upheld the Deputy Chief Constable will make a decision on what further action to take.

6. An explanation or apology will probably be sent to you if the officer concerned is given a formal warning.

7. Where an officer is charged with a disciplinary offence the Chief Constable will conduct a hearing, where you may be allowed to be present to testify, although you may be excluded from those parts of the hearing in which you are not called to speak.

8. You will be informed if you are successful, although no details will be given regarding the penalty imposed. In the event that you are unsuccessful you will be notified by letter.

The decision made by the Deputy Chief Constable is not subject to appeal.

Note that a police investigation is only completed once all charges have been examined.

Criminal Proceedings

Ordinary members of the public are not normally permitted to initiate criminal proceedings. If your complaint to the Chief Constable claims you have been a victim of criminal behaviour on the part of a police officer it will be up to the Procurator Fiscal to decide whether to act on your behalf. The procedure is as follows:

1. Your complaint to the Chief Constable will be passed to the Deputy Chief Constable. It will then pass to the Procurator Fiscal who decides what further action is appropriate.

2. The Procurator Fiscal or a police officer acting on his behalf will interview you.

3. The Procurator Fiscal, generally following consultation with

the Crown Office, will then decide whether to prosecute the officer involved.

4. Should a decision to prosecute be taken the trial will be held in the ordinary criminal court, where you are likely to be called as a witness.

Where allegations of criminal misconduct have been made the police may decide to conduct their own investigation, even if the Procurator Fiscal decides not to prosecute. The procedure is broadly similar to that outlined above under Lesser Offences.

Glossary

by Rita Goddard

ABH
Assault which causes actual bodily harm.

ACPO
Association of Chief Police Officers.

AFO
Authorized firearms officer: a police officer who has been trained in the use of firearms and is authorized to use them.

Architects' Liaison Officer
A police officer whose primary task is to liaise with planning departments, architects and other interested parties in an effort to design new buildings and refurbish old ones in such a way as to minimize crime opportunities.

ARV
Armed Response Vehicle: a police vehicle which is permanently equipped with firearms and is manned by AFOs.

ASU
Administrative Support Unit: duties involve undertaking police administrative duties, including the preparation of case papers.

Bail Jumping
Failing to surrender to bail.

Beat Officer
A police officer who regularly patrols a particular area, or 'beat', either by bicycle or on foot.

Bilking
Dishonestly making off having failed to pay for goods or services.

Breaking and Entering
Term formerly used for burglary, now obsolete.

Burglary
Illegal entry into a building of any type with intent to steal or commit rape, or grevious bodily harm, or unlawful damage.

Butler-Sloss Report
Enquiry report which made recommendations about the response of police and other agencies to reports of child abuse.

Civilianization
The process whereby civilians carry out administrative functions within police establishments, allowing more police to be available for other duties.

Clear-up
According to the Home Office: 'Broadly, an offence is said to be cleared up if a person has been charged, summonsed or cautioned for the offence ... if the offence is admitted and is taken into consideration by the court or, in some cases, if there is sufficient evidence to charge a person but the case is not proceeded with ... The clear-up rate is the ratio of offences cleared up in a year to offences recorded in the year. Some offences cleared up in one year will have been recorded in the previous year.' It should be noted that it is not a prerequisite for someone to have been found guilty in a court for a crime to be 'cleared up'. Clear-up is sometimes also called 'detection'.

Command and Control System
System, often computerized, which records calls for service and availability to respond.

Common Police Services
Centrally provided police support service, e.g. the National Police Computer and the Forensic Science Service.

Computer Crime/White Collar Crime
Whilst no firm description exists, this is generally associated with some types of fraud and forgery.

Consultative Groups
Committees and groups whose aim is to foster good relations between the police and the local community.

Core Subjects/Issues
The topics which are to be inspected within a force in any year.

Counting Rules
Rules provided by the Home Office to all forces to ensure there is parity between the crime statistics of different forces.

Crime Pattern Analysis
   The detailed analysis of crime patterns and trends to help the
   police in their planning.
Crime Prevention Officers
   Whilst crime prevention is the responsibility of all police
   officers some have special responsibility. Advising the public
   and fellow police officers on security and on liaison between
   the police and the local community comprises a large part of
   their duties.
Crown Prosecution Service (CPS)
   The independent national body which is responsible for the
   prosecution of offenders.
Designated Station
   A police station that is designated as suitable for the detention
   of prisoners as required by the Police and Criminal Evidence
   Act.
Detached Beat Officers
   Officers permanently designated to an area which, because of
   its location, is serviced by them directly from their home in
   that area.
Divisions/Sub-divisions
   The main groups into which police forces are divided for
   administrative and/or operational purposes.
Drugs Profit Confiscation Unit
   Unit whose task is to identify the means by which the profits of
   convicted drug dealers can be tracked down and confiscated.
Establishment
   The maximum number of staff a force is permitted by the
   Home Office.
Family of Forces
   A group of forces with similar characteristics, used internally
   by the police for their own performance assessments. In North
   Wales, for example, the 'family' consits of Cleveland, Dorset,
   Durham, Norfolk, North Wales and North Yorkshire.
Field Intelligence Unit
   Officers or unit engaged upon the active gathering of infor-
   mation relating to criminals.
Firearms Teams
   Authorized firearms officers who have received extra specialist

firearms training, normally used as the police's main resource for firearms incidents.

Forensic Science Laboratory
Forensic science service provided by the Home Office to the police.

GBH
Causing grievous bodily harm.

Graded Response
Analysis of calls from the public to ensure an appropriate response, that is immediate or delayed, and to ensure the best use of available resources.

Graduate Entry Scheme
This national scheme offers accelerated promotion prospects to graduates. Only a small proportion of those who join the police are accepted on to the scheme.

Hijacking
Unlawful assumption of control of an occupied aircraft or vehicle (although the Hijacking Act 1971 refers to aircraft alone).

HOLMES
Home Office Large Major Enquiry System: powerful computerized system used for major enquiries.

Hooliganism
Rowdy and disorderly group behaviour in public.

Hostage Taking/Holding
False imprisonment of third party to strengthen claim of bargaining position.

Housebreaking
Burglary.

Informal Resolution
Process by which some complaints against the police can, provided the complainant agrees, be settled at a local level, avoiding the need for a full investigation.

Lay Visitors
Those members of the public or Police Authority authorized to visit police station detention areas on an unscheduled basis.

Multi-Agency
A co-ordinated response by voluntary and statutory agencies, for example police, victim support, social services.

Mutual Aid
System whereby police forces provide police manpower to another force for specific purposes.

NAVSS
National Association of Victim Support Schemes.

National Drug Intelligence Unit (NDIU)
A national unit which collates information on drug offences and offenders.

Neighbourhood Watch
Scheme under which individuals in a locality join together to watch out for local crime.

PACE
Police and Criminal Evidence Act, 1984. Many aspects of police work are governed by this act, in particular the questioning and detention procedures for those helping the police with their enquiries.

Patrol Officers
Officers assigned to operational patrol in uniform, on foot, bicycle or car (not traffic officers).

Pickpocketing
Theft from the person.

Police Authority/Committee
A committee which comprises one-third local magistrates and two-thirds members of the local community. Their function is to secure the maintenance of an adequate and efficient local police force.

Police Complaints Authority (PCA)
An independent body which monitors and supervises the investigation of complaints against the police.

Police Federation
National body representing the interests of police officers up to and including the rank of Chief Inspector.

PNC
Police National Computer.

Police Support Unit (PSU)
A standard unit of police officers comprising one inspector, three sergeants and eighteen constables.

Policing by Objectives
Process whereby objectives are agreed, established and met

through the implementation of locally based action plans and formal evaluation.

Probationary Period
The first two years of a police officer's career.

Public Order Training
Specialized training, comprising three levels, to equip police officers to deal with public disorder.

Regional Crime Squads
Police units comprising officers from a number of adjacent forces, who combine to render more effective investigations that overlap regional boundaries.

Scenes of Crime Officers
Police staff, generally civilian, who collect forensic information at places where a crime has been committed.

Shoplifting
Theft from shops.

Smuggling
Evasion of customs seizure or duty.

Squatting
Whilst entering and remaining on premises is not in itself a criminal offence, it becomes so in a number of circumstances, principally where a trespasser refuses to leave on being requested to do so by a displaced residential occupier.

Staff Associations
The Association of Chief Police Officers, the Superintendents' Association and the Police Federation.

Strength
The actual number of police officers in a force, as distinct from its authorized establishment (see above).

Sub-Divisional Commanders
Superintendents or chief inspectors in charge of sub-divisions.

Support Group
Uniformed officers who perform duty as part of a unit supporting patrol officers at times of public disorder or at special events, or to assist divisional or sub-divisional initiatives.

Taken into Consideration (TIC)
Offences with which an offender is not charged but which are admitted and taken into consideration by the court when sentencing.

Vandalism
Criminal damage.
Victim Suites
Specially equipped rooms which are set aside for the accommodation of victims of crime for interviewing purposes.
Victim Support Schemes
Locally based schemes which offer support and guidance to victims of crime.

Answers to Quiz

Give yourself one point for every correct answer. However, for questions in which you are asked to place things in rank order, one point is awarded for each correct place in the ranking. Thus, if all four items are in correct order you get four points, etc.

1. b. 1 in 3. This may surprise many people yet a Home Office study, released in 1989, found that approximately a third of males born in 1953 had been convicted of a criminal offence before the age of 31. Only a very small proportion of them had committed large numbers of offences. Score 1 point.
2. False. In 1990, of 250,000 violent crimes recorded by the police, 1.4% were rape offences. Rape is an important crime but is heavily over-emphasized by the media and certain pressure groups. The extent of domestic rape, which has only recently become a recognized offence, remains unknown. Score 1 point.
3. b. less vulnerable. Although their hinges are exposed they are harder to force because of their natural direction of movement. Score 1 point.
4. b. strangulation. Score 1 point.
5. b. spouse, cohabitant or former spouse or cohabitant. Score 1 point.
6. High risk: b. Ford Escort Mark 1. Medium risk: c. Ford Escort Mark 3 and d. Porsche 911. Low risk: a. Triumph Dolomite. Score 1 point for each correct ranking, up to a maximum of 4 points.
7. d. airgun, a. pistol, b. sawn-off shot-gun, c. rifle. An enormous number of criminal offences involves the use of airguns (this excludes licensing offences). Score 1 point for each correct ranking, up to a maximum of 4 points.
8. c. at home.
   Score 1 point.

9. b. men aged 16–24 are far more likely to be attacked in the street than any other sector of the population. For every one female assault victim there are at least two males. The disparity is probably even higher as there is considerable evidence that men are less willing to report attacks than women.
Score 1 point.

10. a. 0.2%
Score 1 point.

11. b. fell by 17%. Much of the increase in recorded sexual offences over the decade was probably due to increased reporting and also to changes in police recording practices. The effects of these changes may now be levelling off.
Score 1 point.

12. False. Car-park tickets may tell potential thieves when you entered the car-park and when you plan to leave.
Score 1 point.

13. a. 14–20 years.
Score 1 point.

14. b. 1% Sexual offences receive huge publicity and this distorts public perceptions of what is actually a low risk.
Score 1 point.

15. a. 5+. There are fewer restrictions on alcohol consumption than most people imagine.
Score 1 point.

Maximum score: 21 points;
15–21 very good;
10–14 good;
1–9 poor.

Reference Section

by Rita Goddard

Adfam
(Offers support and advice to parents and friends of drug users)
tel: 071 405 3923

Age Concern
Astral House
1268 London Road
London
SW16 4EJ
tel: 081 679 8000

All Wales Drugsline (Provides advice and information)
1, Neville Street,
Cardiff
CF1 8LP
tel: 0222 383313

Association of British Insurers
51 Gresham Street
London
EC2V 7HQ
tel: 071 600 3333

Audit Commission (researches police efficiency and performance indicators)
1 Vincent Street
London
SW1P 2PF
tel: 071 828 1212

British Standards Institution
2 Park Street
London
W1
tel: 071 629 9000

Chartered Institute of Public Finance and Accountancy (Provides police data)
3 Robert Street
London WC2N 6BH
tel: 071 895 8823

Childline (for children under threat)
tel: 0800 1111
(freephone)

Crime Concern
Level 8 North
Brunel Tower
David Murray John Building
Swindon
Wilts
SN1 1LY
tel: 0793 514596

Families Need Fathers (advises fathers about general legal and social issues)
B. M. Families
London
WC1N 3XX
tel: 081 886 0970

Freephone Drug Problems
Dial 100 and ask operator for this freephone advice service

Health and Safety Executive
Information Centre
Broad Lane
Sheffield
S3 7HQ
tel: 0742 892345

Institute for the Study of Drug Dependence
1 Hatton Place
Hatton Garden
London EC1N 8ND
tel: 071 430 1991

Joint Council for the Welfare of Immigrants
115 Old Street
London
EC1V 9JR
tel: 071 251 8706

London Rape Crisis Centre
P O Box 69
London WC1
tel: 071 916 5466
    071 837 1600
for Scotland tel: 031 556 9437

London Women's Aid
52–54 Featherstone Street
London
EC1Y 8RT
tel: 071 251 6537

National Council for Civil Liberties
21 Tabard Street
London
SE1 4LA
tel: 071 403 3888

National Society for the Prevention of Cruelty to Children
Saffron Hill
London
EC1
tel: 071 242 1626

Nuisance Phonecalls
General advice (recorded message)
tel: 0800 666700 (freephone)
Special Investigations
tel: 0800 661441

Parents Against Injustice
(gives advice, counselling and support to parents, children, family members, professional carers and others when a child is mistakenly thought to be at risk or to have been abuse)
3 Riverside Business Park
Stanstead
Essex
CM24 8PL
tel: 0279 647171

Police Complaints Authority
10 Great George Street
London
SW1P 3AE
tel: 071 273 6450

Police Federation
15/17 Langley Road
Surbiton
Surrey
KT6 6LP
tel: 081 399 2224

Release – National Legal and Drugs Services
388 Old Street
London
EC1V 9LT
Advice Line: 071 729 9904
Emergency Help Line: 071 603 8654

Royal Scottish Society for the Prevention of Cruelty to Children
41 Polwarth Terrace
Edinburgh
EH11 1NU
tel: 031 337 8539

Scottish Council for Civil Liberties
146 Holland Street
Glasgow
G2 4NG
tel: 041 332 5960

SCODA (Standing Conference on Drug Abuse)
1 Hatton Place
London EC1N 8ND
tel: 071 430 2341

Scottish Drugs Forum
266 Clyde Street
Glasgow
G1 4JH
tel: 041 221 1175

Suzy Lamplugh Trust
14 East Sheen Avenue
London
SW14 8AS
tel: 081 392 1839

Thatcham Motor Insurance Repair Research Centre
Colthrop Lane
Thatcham
Newbury
Berkshire
RG13 4NP
tel: 0635 868855

Victim Support
National Office
Cranmer House
39 Brixton Road
London
SW9 6DD
tel: 071 735 9166